RUNNING

AROUND

TOWN

AN
ANN ARBOR
MEMOIR

STEPHEN K. POSTEMA

Fifth Avenue Press is a locally focused and publicly owned publishing imprint of the Ann Arbor District Library. It is dedicated to supporting the local writing community by promoting the production of original fiction, nonfiction, and poetry written for children, teens, and adults.

First Printing 2025

Cover and book design: Nathaniel Roy
Editor: Emily Murphy

ISBN: 978-1-956697-48-3 (Paperback)

Fifth Avenue Press
343 S. Fifth Ave
Ann Arbor, MI 48104
fifthavenue.press

For Chrissy.

"Life can only be understood backwards; but it must be lived forwards."

—SØREN KIERKEGAARD

CONTENTS

MUSICAL
REFERENCES

INTRODUCTION

THESE ESSAYS ARE ABOUT GROWING UP in Ann Arbor, Michigan, during the 1960s and 1970s. The Counterculture Era. The Vietnam War Era. The Civil Rights Era. The "Me" Decade. The Age of Disillusionment. During those decades, Ann Arbor absorbed so many people, ideas, and events, that I knew, even as a boy, I was living in a unique and formative time and place in history. The decade of the 1960s alone saw Ann Arbor increase in population by an astounding 50 percent.

And they were formative years for me. In 1963, our family arrived in Ann Arbor during the city's rapid growth, and I left for college in 1977. I write about these years now because the images remain vivid as I attempt to capture a sense of place with words and perspective that I did not have at the time. I write to understand my past.

Much later in life, I was interviewed about my hometown and was asked if it was true that Ann Arbor has always been "twenty square miles surrounded by reality." I had to correct the interviewer: Ann Arbor is 29.09 square miles. As to its reputation for being unreal, Ann Arbor was more like a constant social experiment: a crazy compression chamber of societal forces.

My world was centered on the southwest quadrant of the city; it extended from our home in a modest neighborhood to downtown Ann Arbor and the University of Michigan campus, where my father was the pastor of a student chapel a block off the central Diag—*smack dab in the middle of all the action.*

These essays capture personal interactions with some of the people

Aerial photo of University of Michigan Diag. Smack dab in the middle of town. Aerial view from 1942, University Planner's Office (University of Michigan) Records, 1940-2014, Box 47, Aerials, 1956-2002, Bentley Historical Library, University of Michigan.

I met during this time. A girl who suggested I pay more attention to life. A boy who gave sartorial advice in the Fuller Pool locker room. The cashiers at Discount Records. A clerk at the Middle Earth store on campus. Random interactions were transformative.

And there were more: The teachers who pushed and prodded, and dangled extra credit in exchange for writing about current events. A neighbor who was a policeman and bailed me out of "situational predicaments," as he termed them. Another neighbor who was a congressman—a close friend of the future President Ford—who kept me informed on political matters. A coach who encouraged a broadened horizon. And importantly, a girl who passed me a note in history class.

These interactions had a cumulative effect on me. Sometimes they changed the trajectory of my life.

These essays also touch on three basics for me—baked goods, basketball, and books—as well as various obsessions of mine: mathematics, excellent handwriting, and current events.

I was in a hurry during these times and loved to run. I ran—first, out of fear; later, as a way to keep from exploding as a teenager, as a way to channel a serious need to compete, and also, gradually, as a way to watch my town.

Music held the 1960s and 1970s together. I observed these decades with a backdrop of music—folk, rock, soul, and jazz—initially listening from a small, white transistor radio, then an old red 45 rpm record player, and then a used brown Lloyd's stereo with small Advent speakers. Today, just hearing a beat or some words of a song can bring me clearly back to an event, a snippet of conversation, a trauma, or a kind word.

The music of those times that had pulsated throughout Ann Arbor brings back the memories of the days I ran around this town.

CHAPTER 1
1969-1970

The Year Away from Ann Arbor

AS AN OVERTURE TO THESE ESSAYS, I begin unconventionally in the middle with our family leaving Ann Arbor for a year in 1969. I had lived in Ann Arbor for almost seven years when we left, and I would be there for seven more years after we got back, before leaving for college.

1969. Two mind-bending enterprises were being planned for that summer: the first moon landing by Apollo 11 and the Woodstock music festival. Layered on top of these events, the U.S. government was planning to begin the selective service draft for the Vietnam War effort. The Vietnam War permeated all aspects of life. Every night, beginning in 1967, the body court of the war was revealed on the news.

Yet many wanted peace. The United States Supreme Court had even held that students had a constitutional right to wear black armbands with a peace sign to school to protest the Vietnam War. I had read about the case in the newspaper: *Tinker v. Des Moines Independent Community School District*. (And, as all things relate back to Ann Arbor, the youngest of the *Tinker* children who wore the armband to elementary school eventually moved to Ann Arbor and opened a Birkenstock shoe store.)

Closer to home, in the midst of the turmoil, my father was plan-

The Postema Family in 1967. I am the boy with the tilted head.

ning to take a sabbatical to Berkeley, California, for the 1969–70 school year. His fantastical scheme was revealed piecemeal: Our family, with four kids ages three to eleven, would drive our blue Ford station wagon to Berkeley with a five-thousand-mile detour to Cuernavaca, Mexico, (the site of a conference my father was to attend). The car would pull a pop-up Coleman tent camper across the country and through Mexico.

The total trip would take over two months and around seventy-five hundred miles. It sounded spectacular. The downside: each kid could take only the clothes and possessions that they could stuff into one cardboard beer carton (the size of four six-packs) obtained from the downtown Beer Depot. Mine was a Stroh's beer carton.

Two nights into the trip, in June 1969, my father called back to Ann Arbor and found out that the city was in the midst of what would become one of the largest student protests in the city's history. He wondered whether there was any damage to the student chapel, as it had a central location on campus.

A solid limestone building with beautiful stained-glass windows,

16

the Campus Chapel, built in the 1940s, was located just a block over from South University Ave., where some of the rioting began. As we headed down the highway, my mom worried about the chaos and wondered aloud whether, in the coming year, Berkeley would be a little more peaceful than Ann Arbor.

When we arrived in Berkeley two months later with no housing lined up, my father found a place to park the camper: off a busy street near campus, in a parking lot that had been converted into temporary camping for people living on the streets. (It would be like setting up a campsite in Ann Arbor on the concrete pavement of the once-empty Budget Rent a Car lot near the University of Michigan campus.) Nevertheless, one morning, when I stumbled out of the camper and surveyed the street action in Berkeley, the upbeat, recent hit song "Aquarius/Let the Sunshine In" by The 5th Dimension came to mind.

But living with a street view of the day-to-day life in "The Age of Aquarius" was not ideal. When I went to get my mom a newspaper that morning, the headlines reported that there was someone called the "Zodiac" serial killer on the loose in the Bay Area, and the paper also had further details of a crazed Charles Manson cult in Southern California that was at large and possibly moving north.

I debated whether to tell my mom they were out of papers, as I knew she would not take this news very well, particularly because the little lock on our camper door was now broken. But I handed the paper over and watched her absorb this information. That very afternoon, my parents found a house in Richmond, about eight miles from the Berkeley campus. Before school each day, my brother reminded me that the Zodiac Killer might be in the neighborhood.

So I ran to school.

And running was second nature to me. In our subdivision in Ann Arbor, many houses on Covington Dr. had signs depicting blue "helping hands" in the window. As explained to me in kindergarten in 1964, these houses were places of refuge for kids who encountered trouble while away from their own homes. But I wasn't paying attention carefully and thought these homes were homes of bad people. So I would run past them quickly.

Over time, I got clarification on this situation: We lived in a safe area, and the houses with these signs were not a danger. There were just a lot of helpful parents in the neighborhood, mostly moms, who put these signs up because they were around during the day. But because there were so many of these signs in the neighborhood, my young mind just assumed the Dicken school area where we lived was a magnet for predators. Plus, the blue, disembodied hands themselves were somewhat creepy.

So I continued to run. Everywhere.

During the first week of school in Richmond, California—at ten years old and in fifth grade—I found myself surrounded on the way home by a group of kids who demanded to know why I was in their territory and where I was from. I did what so many from Michigan would do: I raised my right hand with my fingers held close together so it looked like the state of Michigan.

"I'm from Ann Arbor, Michigan," I said as I pointed at the approximate location of where Ann Arbor was on the right-hand map. A little context for them about the hand-map concept might have worked better. The group looked puzzled.

In hindsight, my repeated jabbing of my finger into my hand may have been taken as some sort of gesture of disrespect or a Michigan gang symbol. They took offense. Derision followed, then hostility.

"I come from a peace-loving family," I called out, showing them the silver peace-sign ring I was wearing on my middle finger (because it was a little large for my ring finger). This just made matters worse.

"I'll take that ring and your finger," one of the kids said while pulling out a knife.

I fled and did not look back. I found that all my years of running had prepared me very well for this exact moment. All I remember thinking as I ran home was: Why were there no blue helping hands here in California?

The next day, the principal transferred me to another school after my parents took me into his office to describe the warm welcome I had received on school property. He asked me some questions. He didn't appreciate my suggestion that he pay greater attention to safety on school property. My mention that I had recently purchased a very large hunting knife in Colorado (a fact that was also news to my parents at that time) seemed to raise eyebrows all around. In any case, I was sent to another school even farther away.

So I ran even faster and longer.

But I loved the new school. There were kids of many ethnicities and religions: African-American, Hispanic, Japanese, Brazilian, Chinese, Filipino, Indian, Russian, German; Mormon, Jewish, Buddhist, Shinto, Baptist, and Catholic. Years later, I found out that Richmond was one of the most diverse cities in the country. My best friend was from a large Mormon family, and he taught me about the social and cultural dimensions of this new place.

We spent much of the year studying United States geography, with each student having to write a lengthy state report. As a new student from another state, I was treated as an expert on the state of Michigan. I was called upon to dispense information about anything related to Michigan. And I used all the knowledge of Michigan history that I had just learned the prior year in fourth grade—filled in with creative descriptions and other facts that seemed to emerge as reality whenever I began to speak.

I told the class of the wonders of Michigan. I said that the Great Lakes had virtues above all bodies of water and that Michigan had the longest coastline in the lower United States and the largest freshwater coastline of anywhere in the world. I repeated that the largest and most beautiful sand dunes were at the Sleeping Bear Dunes.

I elaborated upon details about the largest cereal factory in the world, the Kellogg's cereal factory in Battle Creek, which gave away a free snack pack of cereals upon a visit. And I gave them intricate details of the largest stadium in the world, the University of Michigan football stadium, which was nearly in my backyard. I had seen them all.

I was a proselytizer for the state of Michigan and my hometown. No matter what Michigan topic, I found that I had things to add. Furniture production in Grand Rapids. The auto industry in Detroit. I even waxed poetic about the delicious fall Michigan apples and summer South Haven peaches and Traverse City cherries.

And I spoke of the Michigan-made Vernors ginger ale and Faygo Red Pop as if they were the true elixirs of life. The teacher seemed rather skeptical about some of the information I was providing to the class. But she didn't stop me.

So I kept going.

The girl who was assigned to report on the state of Michigan sought me out for my expertise, and she invited me to her house after school. I was treated with great hospitality. Her family had come from Japan. Her mother gave us rice crackers and cold barley tea.

My classmate laid the "M" volume of the World Book Encyclopedia open to a map of Michigan. I laid my right hand palm side up over the encyclopedia map and carefully showed her how the hand map could be a valuable geographical descriptor.

I showed her where Ann Arbor was and told her everything I could about my city. Details such as our house on Covington Dr., the U.S. Congressman who lived a few doors down, the candy counter at Drake's Sandwich Shop, the public library bookmobile, the Huron River, the Arboretum, and the University of Michigan campus.

With her little brother and mother looking on, I pointed to Ann Arbor on the map on the page and then on my hand map. They were quite interested in this.

My classmate included some of the information I had provided in her fifty-three-page Michigan report, with a detailed section devoted to the importance of the city of Ann Arbor. She had beautiful handwriting. During her class presentation, I sat back proudly as she raised her own hand and pointed out Ann Arbor on her open palm.

My last day at school, I said goodbye to my classmates. The girl I had helped with her Michigan report was the last person I spoke to before I left. She waved goodbye with her right hand. Then she held her hand in the shape of Michigan. "A great state," she said, smiling, adding: "The Wolverine State. Population 8,875,000."

She pointed to her right-hand map of Michigan:

"Ann Arbor, right here. You'll be home soon."

CHAPTER 2
September 1963

Home: 1810 Covington

THE ENORMOUS WHITE OAK TREE in Mushroom Park was already over two hundred years old when I first saw it as a child. We had moved into our house, five houses from the park, on Covington Drive in Ann Arbor in September of 1963. I was told that the tree was much older than the city, indeed older than the United States of America. The tree itself, and its slow and winding growth, made me think of the history of Ann Arbor often when I was young. Fortunately, it had been spared from removal when our subdivision was built. I spent a great deal of time under that tree with a book, sometimes reading about the history of Ann Arbor.

The founders of Ann Arbor, John Allen and Elisha Rumsey, registered a plat of land in 1824. They were dreamers and avid promoters of the city, and described it as a "promised land."

Ann Arbor existed before Michigan became a state. In fact, in December 1836, it was in Ann Arbor that delegates from the Michigan territory gathered in a courthouse building (where the current Washtenaw County courthouse now stands, on the corner of Main St. and Huron St.) and voted for Michigan to become a state.

Other residents also promoted the city, and in 1837, it gained the prize of the University of Michigan; just thirty years later, U-M was one the largest universities, public or private, in the United States.

1810 Covington, 1967. Postema siblings and cousins.

Thus, promises, dreams, and growth were part of Ann Arbor's history from the start.

And the promise of Ann Arbor was nowhere near as evident as when the city's population grew the fastest. It grew from forty-eight thousand to one hundred thousand in only two decades—from 1950 to 1970—with an astonishing thirty-three-thousand-person gain during the decade of the 1960s alone. To put this into perspective, the city's population grew by only twenty thousand in the next fifty years, from 1970 to 2020. The engine for this remarkable growth was the University of Michigan, an increase in scientific research jobs, and the post-war baby boom.

To help accommodate this growth, in the mid-1950s and 1960s, in the southwest corner of Ann Arbor, cornfields were transformed into an expanding subdivision in four parts, known as the Vernon Downs subdivision. Covington Dr. was the longest street in the subdivision (almost 0.6 miles long). Covington ran north–south, starting in a court at the top of a hill and gently declining for over a half mile until it ended at Scio Church Road, which was then a dirt road. Across Scio Church Rd. sat an abandoned and overgrown cornfield with a barn and outbuildings that remained into the 1970s, a reminder of what the land had once been.

The Postema family, with four children, was part of this exponential growth of the city. Our family arrived in Ann Arbor in 1963 from Amsterdam, where my father had been doing postgraduate studies. My father took a position as pastor at Campus Chapel, a student chapel on the central University of Michigan campus and four miles from our house.

And though the church owned our house, my parents made this standard brick quad-level a home. The kitchen and attached dining room were a focal point. This was my mother's domain. Our home had the scent of baked goods. My very tall great-grandfather had emigrated from the Netherlands and established a Dutch bakery in Pella, Iowa, in 1896, which still operates today under his name: Vander Ploeg Bakery. My mother was an excellent baker and made cookies, rolls of many kinds, pies, and importantly, breads made out of anything—apples to zucchinis, and everything in between. She had the discipline of a baker's daughter, arising early to mix, knead, and place dough in the oven.

She could also transform even the saddest piece of bruised fruit into something of sublime taste and comfort.

Sometimes, while something was in the oven, she would come out the back door, still in her apron, and play basketball with me in the driveway. She had played basketball in high school in Iowa, where women's basketball was a very popular pastime. And she was a very good shot. "Remember to follow your shot," she reminded me often.

My mother had taught elementary school after college and then became a part-time substitute teacher. She was particularly good at math, and she kept track of the limited finances of our family with confident and precise calculations. She could find a bargain at any store, and she furnished our home with savvy purchases from the Treasure Mart, a beloved thrift store. She set the pace of life in our house, like a steady heartbeat.

Another central place in the house was my father's study.

Two of my grandparents had only completed eighth grade; one, tenth grade; and one, high school, yet all four of my grandparents (all Dutch) liked to read, and education was a primary focus in our family. My father was a Fulbright Scholar in Amsterdam for three years after college and seminary, studying pastoral psychology. And he had been encouraged in this venture by a powerful man whom I would follow over time because of a letter I had stumbled upon while rummaging through one of the drawers in the study's desk. It was a letter, dated April 25, 1960, from Michigan Congressman Gerald Ford that said "May I congratulate you on this Fulbright honor and wish you every success in the Netherlands ... If there is anything I can do to assist you ... please feel free to contact me any time ... Warmest personal regards."

By the time of his retirement, my father's study held several thousand books (on an elaborate set of jerry-rigged shelves that only my father and brother knew how to construct and deconstruct). He had magazines of every kind, especially those with great photographs such as *Life* and *Look*. A burgundy leather chair sat in the corner. It was a great chair to read in, and I would feel smarter just sitting in it.

But it was also where we had to sit when we were in trouble and instructed to reflect about some transgression or other. And there were many transgressions in my case. I might as well just confess up front that many of these transgressions arose because I simply didn't fully appreciate the laws related to trespassing on property. I believed that the city, the schools, and the U-M buildings were public property. I further believed that they were seriously underutilized, particularly after hours.

The various authorities in this city clearly saw it differently.

And even after this was pointed out to me, it didn't quite stick. In my young mind, what was the point of saying "forgive us our trespasses" every Sunday in church if you had not actually trespassed during the week? I compiled a list of the places I had trespassed to confess each week and receive forgiveness for. So I had to sit in this chair a lot.

This was quite fine with me, except for one detail.

On the wall near this chair was a 1964 *Time* magazine cover featuring the Reverend Dr. Martin Luther King Jr. My father was an ardent admirer, and after he went to Washington, D.C., to hear him speak in early 1968, my father added another picture of Reverend King, one with piercing eyes and a soulful look, captioned "What Are You Doing with Your Life?" I could disappoint my parents; I could disappoint my teachers and principals; I could disappoint a purportedly omniscient God, but having to sit in the chair and face the Reverend Dr. Martin Luther King Jr. was exceedingly difficult. And transformative. No matter where I looked from the chair, his eyes were upon me, urging a purposeful life and sense of priorities.

And while Rev. King watched over my father's study and those who sat in the burgundy chair during the 1960s and 1970s, we, in turn, watched a time of turmoil as the city, the state, and the nation sought purpose and priorities.

And Sunday in our home was a day for reflection and reading and church. Such reflection for me, from a young age, required poring over the Sunday *Ann Arbor News* and the *Detroit Free Press* between morning and evening church services. The papers provided unlimited and obscure things to think about on Sundays. I gradually read every section, including the comics, advice columns, classifieds, obituaries, and importantly, the list of top forty songs of the week.

Music. Another thing in our house influenced our reflections and worldview: our upright piano and the music it created. Both of my parents played the piano, and we were raised on all the great hymns produced throughout history. The hymns I liked best were gospel music. Gospel was a short leap to the soul music, blues, and folk music of the 1960s. Then on to rock. So I listened to music very carefully. I flipped through the record bins at Discount Records, a store near campus. I became obsessed with the song "Blowin' in the Wind" by Bob Dylan, which framed the challenges of the 1960s.

But even with the challenges of these times, the solutions were also clearly laid out early for me in May of 1964, at a place almost in our backyard. One only had to go a short way down Scio Church Rd., then up Main Street to find the largest college football stadium in the country. It was there, on that day in 1964, that President Lyndon B. Johnson came to speak at U-M's commencement. I was excited because my mother had told us the president was coming. And I thought she meant to our house. But it was close enough.

The president came to Ann Arbor to lay out his vision of the Great Society.

"Will you join in the battle to build the Great Society, to prove that our material progress is only the foundation on which we will build a richer life of mind and spirit?"

Seventy-five thousand people listened on. President Johnson called on the government and ordinary citizens (particularly young people) to envision a just society, free from the evils of racism and poverty.

He exhorted the students: "For better or for worse, your generation has been appointed by history to deal with those problems and to lead America toward a new age ... You can help build a society where the demands of morality, and the needs of the spirit, can be realized in the life of the Nation."

It sounded like a religious revival meeting when my father described it.

My father, who was not quite thirty years old, had attended the speech, and he read us these, and other, excerpts the next day after dinner. "The demands of morality, and the needs of the spirit," my father repeated. And, as if the president had spoken directly to him, my father said: "There is a lot of work to do," and went up to his study. The Postema children at that time were seven, five, and three, and we looked at each other. We were used to such pronouncements.

And while we contemplated that we were evidently appointed by history to lead America, according to the president of the United States, we still needed dessert.

My mother brought us warm banana bread.

CHAPTER 3

1965

Locations and Names

A STRANGE THING ABOUT GROWING UP on Covington Dr. was that many of the street names in the subdivision were names of English towns or names from English History. Our house on Covington was near Barrington, Glastonbury, Saxon, Waltham, Brampton Court, and Warwick Court. Agincourt and Windsor were next door on either side. And at the top of Covington was Runnymeade, where Dicken Elementary School sat. These names eventually encouraged me to look them up in our red 1945 edition of the World Book Encyclopedia. But even as a boy, I thought the English names were a bit much for a neighborhood of small brick houses, many of which had a flagpole and flew the American flag regularly—perhaps as a daily reminder of the American victory in the Revolutionary War.

And heading north on Runnymede, just before it dead-ended into a trail to the business district on Stadium, was a funny intersection of streets: Stephen Terrace, Carol Drive, and Sue Parkway. These ordinary names converged on Runnymede, the name for the birthplace of the Magna Carta in England.

Of course, for the Postema siblings named Stephen, Carol, and Sue, we thought this was of grand—even cosmic—significance. My brother Tom was left out of this convergence, but even he was amused by it.

"They are just names," he said.

Postema siblings, 1968. From left to right: Tom, Carol, Sue, and me.

Yes, but our names.

These street names caused us to inquire more about the origins of our own names, and that lead to a greater understanding of our parents.

Sort of.

It was not only street names that borrowed from the English. Tom was named after the British poet Thomas Stearns Eliot. But instead of "Stearns," his middle name was "Scott." Stearns would have fit him well; he was stern, diligent, and reliable from a young age, with a love for the discipline of classical and choral music. He could carefully construct intricate car or spacecraft models, purchased from Rider's Hobby Shop, all the way through to the last decals.

My father then took this academic naming in a convoluted direction with me. Much to my surprise, my name was inspired by Søren Kierkegaard, the theologian, philosopher, and writer. My father was a big fan of his writing and really wanted me, his second son, to have the initials "S. K."

Rather than name me "Soren," which was nixed by my mother, my parents evidently agreed on "Stephen," after the Saint or an uncle or both. The "S" name made some sense.

But as to the "K," it became muddled. When I found this out, even at a young age I had to wonder what wine or other alcohol they were drinking to explain this. The fact is, my parents could not think of a name they had liked that started with "K," so they used the name of the county I was born in, and I became "Stephen Kent." It could have been worse, I suppose. I could have been born in Kalkaska County.

My mother, to prevent further literary naming, took over the naming of my sisters and used primarily family names, beginning with Carol Ann for both grandmothers. Carol, who was artistic and empathetic, had a rebellious streak; she would sometimes boycott family game night, which was not understandable to the rest of us avid competitors. She kept confidences well and was supportive of any schemes I was working on.

Susan Beth was named after an aunt and a neighbor, and she was inquisitive, musical, and disciplined. She would draw detailed maps of the nearby fields, where we would walk with our dog, and would listen attentively to my strategic theories about the game Yahtzee as we played into the night at the dining room table.

In any event, given my own naming history, it is not surprising that I had a bond with Kierkegaard and began reading some of his works while sitting in my father's burgundy leather chair in the corner of his study. (Even if I was there for some perceived infraction of social or familial norms.)

And from an early age, I was attracted to Kierkegaard's quote: "Life can only be understood backwards; but it must be lived forwards." The burgundy chair was a chair in which I was encouraged, at times, to reflect, to look backwards at my life to understand it.

But after times of contemplation, we were all encouraged to live life forwards: this meant venturing out from our small subdivision with English-themed street names and into the broader world that was Ann Arbor.

Gradually, I ventured out from our English-themed neighborhood, running or biking. A mile east down Scio Church Rd., there were cross-country running trails in the fields on the southern part of the two-hundred-acre Pioneer High School property, which encompassed the high school, athletic fields, and adjacent nature area and woods. A half-mile north on Main St., going into town, was the iconic University of Michigan football stadium and next to it: Crisler Arena, the basketball stadium and concert venue.

Another mile north was the downtown, which had three other important places: the Ann Arbor Public Library, the YMCA, and Rider's Hobby Shop. Finally, a half-mile east of downtown was the central campus of the University of Michigan. On campus, there were four stores that held particular significance to me: Discount Records, Drake's Sandwich Shop, Middle Earth, and Harrington's Stamp and Coin.

There were times to go west on Scio Church Rd., to go over the highway to the farmland, the countryside, and a large gravel pit for exploration. But the inexorable pull over the years was to the center of town, to the campus, the students, and the unceasing activity on the University of Michigan Diag.

CHAPTER 4
Summer 1967

Allmendinger Park and Warm Tar

GROWING UP IN ANN ARBOR IN THE 1960S, there were many mothers who, by choice or convention, stayed home during the day. Most of them wore dresses and comfortable shoes, and they cooked and baked and would provide lunch and snacks to whoever was around. From a young age, my mom, like many in the neighborhood, only required that you make it home by a set dinner time. While a call at lunch if eating somewhere else was suggested, it was not required.

Other than that, we were pretty much on our own in the summer and on Saturdays. This created an environment where kids roamed free all day, running—sometimes amok—from park to park or to other neighborhoods on their bikes. But they were often in earshot of moms they didn't even know, who would impose order as needed.

Schools and parks offered an abundance of summer activities for children, and the newspaper advertised each park's weekly activities. In 1967, I had turned eight, and having reached that age, my bike range expanded. One morning, I rode my bike to Allmendinger Park (about a mile and a half), wearing a new Batman t-shirt, to check out the action. I hoped to be in time for the scheduled dodgeball tournament.

Parents were absent, but young park counselors were on duty. When I arrived, kids were finishing up their lanyard-braiding projects. The girls had their neat and colorful braids well underway and

Postema siblings on the back porch, 1967. I'm wearing the (in)famous Batman t-shirt.

were engaged in careful conversation. The boys were having trouble concentrating and instead seemed to be more focused on whipping each other with the braids than creating anything.

One thing led to another. Others got involved. Monkey-like throwing of projectiles—from rubber balls to dirt clods. Boys running and dodging. Soon, the fracas began to engulf innocent bystanders like me, although I felt strangely invincible in my Batman shirt. The skirmish migrated to the edge of the park near a street-patching project where the workers were absent, which conveniently provided new ammunition in the form of a still-warm heap of tar near the curb.

As the tar began to find its way into hands and the air, and some in my hair, a mom came out of one of the houses. Wearing a nice dress and apron and brandishing a very large Rubbermaid spatula, she read everyone the riot act. (I lost focus for a moment wondering whether the spatula had just been used in a baking project, and if so, what type of baked goods might be in her house.) She had a commanding presence and demanded that the tar use cease and desist.

This was a mom with strong arms and thick hands who could clearly impose restraint if needed.

"Everyone who touched the tar," she called out, "come right here."

Kids ambled over reluctantly.

"Names and phone numbers," she demanded, holding up the spatula.

She then decreed that those with tar on them had to go home, and she made it clear she would be calling our mothers. To simply run away did not occur to any of the boys. I assumed her orders would not apply to me even though I had tar on my hands, as I had not thrown any tar nor had I instigated the skirmish.

She put her spatula in the apron and pulled out a small red notebook and pen. I admired her preparedness. I believed that she was going to at least go over the facts and make a determination of guilt. And I was looking forward to being exonerated. But as she went down the perp line, recording names and numbers, it became clear that this park mom was going to assume the guilt of everyone involved.

Rather unfair, I thought. But I complied, mumbling a bit, and pausing—I rearranged the last two digits of our phone number. "Are you sure?" she asked about the number, making a note. While I thought she was overly broad in her maintenance of order, I did admire her ability to quell the disturbance.

Rather than go straight home, I eyed the bookmobile sponsored by the public library. It was a large RV that contained a small library and was dispatched to parks and schools over the summer on a fixed schedule. I had a secret project going on that involved sending notes back and forth with commentary about a book. I did not know the person I was corresponding with; they would only sign their notes "T." I wanted to check if there were any further messages in the book. The bookmobile driver looked at the tar on me and just shook his head. Clearly, she was of the same mind as the park mom.

I was used to having grime, dirt, and filth of all derivations on my hands. But tar was a new experience. I rode home trying to figure out the best explanation for the tar. My mom intercepted me before I even made it into the house. "I hear there was a problem at the park," she said. The phone number subterfuge had clearly not been effective. "Why exactly would you get involved in this?"

"Why?" I could only parrot back as I shook my head.

I did explain that things had happened very quickly, that I had

33

been swept up in a matter way beyond my control. My mom viewed self-control differently. "You don't want to let things to get too wild," she would say. But I was conflicted about the term "wild." My mom clearly saw it as a negative, but I had heard on my radio the number one song "Wild Thing" by The Troggs. I felt its meaning was somewhat beyond my comprehension, but I was interested, as the song talked about a wild thing that would cause a heart to sing.

And I liked the phrase. (I learned later that Jimi Hendrix got so excited playing this song at a concert in 1967, when he was only seventeen years old, that he lit his guitar on fire. This fact likely would have been another point of example for my mom had she heard about it.)

But at that moment, my mom focused on another more practical concern: "Where is your new t-shirt?" I went outside and panicked when I checked my bike, remembering then that I had taken it off for the ride home. It must have fallen off somewhere after I had loosely tied it to my bike.

My mom was efficient about the mess that remained, opening up the mineral oil.

Not wasting any time with alternative solutions to tar in the hair, she then got the clippers, took me outside, and gave me a summer buzzcut that I was due for anyway. As for the Batman shirt, I was sent out to retrace my route to find it. And I did, not too far from home. When I got back, I had lunch on the porch, with a new haircut and new clothes, while discussing behavioral expectations with my mom.

She pointedly asked if I actually knew our phone number. I could guess what that was about. And she reiterated a useful rule of returning with all the clothes one had left the house with. I checked the paper to see what was going on at the Dicken and Lawton playgrounds in the afternoon. Tetherball tournaments at both locations.

Very promising in my view.

CHAPTER 5
Late 1960s

Workshops and White Objects

GROWING UP IN THE 1960s in Ann Arbor, I was always interested in what the parents in the neighborhood did for work. And thinking back on the fathers' jobs, tools, cars, a cop's finger, outer space, and Congress come immediately to mind.

But my most immediate memory of the dads in our neighborhood is that most had serious workshops in their basements or garages, with a full array of tools. I envied these collections of molded metallic usefulness and their sheer potential. The Postema family had a rather pathetic assortment of tools in the "junk drawer" of our kitchen. So we, of course, ended up frequently borrowing tools from neighbors and needing their mechanical expertise.

Three houses down lived Chuck Wolfe and his family. He owned the C-Ted's Standard station on South University, in the heart of the campus area near my father's chapel. Mr. Wolfe was reputed to be able to fix any car. He regularly fixed the tired Postema family station wagons at a "clergy" discount. Sometimes, when our car needed more serious overnight attention, he would even give my father a ride home from the station.

Next door to the left, Police Officer Fleming—another Chuck—didn't mind lending us tools from his gleaming collection as long as they came back cleaned, a condition he particularly reminded me

Officer Chuck Fleming keeping track of the Postema children via new radar equipment.
© 1967 MLive Media Group. All Rights Reserved. Used with permission.

about. Officer Fleming had a brush cut, a holdover from previous military service. He sported a white t-shirt outside in the summer and had an extensive workshop in his garage with every tool carefully hung up on the wall like a shrine.

"I'm telling you, things are in decline," he'd say to the audience of kids who would sit on his driveway and watch him fix things in his garage. He would pause and turn to us while holding up a hammer or a wrench to make a point. He had a mission to protect the city. And he had tools to fix things in decline.

He was well-liked by the merchants and students alike. I liked to hear him regale my father with tales about his work policing the city, including performing what I then believed to be the most important task in the city: operating the bullhorn on game days at the intersection of Stadium Boulevard and Main Street, adjacent to the University of Michigan football stadium. This intersection was the key to all movement in the city on football Saturdays. And he was fully in charge.

Nothing was in decline at that intersection.

Officer Fleming watched out for our family, both in the neighborhood and down on campus where he was a beat cop, and we were able to actually aid him one summer day when he came over holding the severed tip of his finger in one hand and a bloody cloth wrapped around his other hand. His lawnmower engine repair project had gone awry. Without missing a beat, my dad put him in the backseat of our car to take him to the emergency room, and my mom calmly got a glass of milk to put his fingertip in. My mom always seemed to know what to do in any situation.

"Could you turn off the radio?" Officer Fleming grimaced as The Beatles' "Revolution" played on the car radio, CKLW AM 800. "And don't worry about the speed limit," he whispered.

I had an important task in all of this. I held the glass very carefully on the way to the hospital and couldn't help but watch the fingertip bobbing in the milk. Luckily, the surgeons were able to stitch his finger back together.

Though Office Fleming always remained concerned about the lack of tools at our house, along with the increased length of our hair over time, he was quite grateful for our prompt emergency assistance. And it showed. Even when he had occasion to chew me out in later years for what he referred to in police jargon as "situational predicaments," he always gestured at me with this fixed finger, a sign I took to mean that he remembered our bond.

A number of the other neighborhood dads with significant workshops (some with elaborate vises that, frankly, deserve their own essays) worked at Bendix Aerospace, where they were involved in the space missions. One friend's description of his father's work for a class project really piqued my interest: "My dad works on a piece of equipment that tracks white objects on moon trips."

I thought a great deal about this but never took the time to find out what it actually meant. I knew about the race between the United States and the Soviet Union to put a man on the moon. Would these objects somehow impede that? I was vaguely concerned about the "white objects" for some time. They seemed very important—after all, they were being tracked.

While I didn't know the workshop status of the family across the street and two doors over, I knew the father was a politician. He was our state representative for a term and then U.S. Congressman for a decade. My parents didn't agree with him on every issue, but Marvin Esch was probably the only Republican congressman my parents ever voted for. My mom liked him because he was kind, a good listener, well-spoken, and thoughtful about policy matters; her view was likely also informed by the fact that my mom considered his children "well-mannered."

My father liked Mr. Esch because of his wide range of interests, his opposition to the Vietnam War, and his focus on education and racial justice. Esch served in the Michigan House of Representatives from 1965 to 1966. In 1966, he was elected to Congress, representing Ann Arbor and southeastern Michigan until 1977. His congressional campaign slogan seems quite radical today: "Thinks for Himself, Works for Us!" He gave me a signed Esch bumper sticker that I kept for some time in my memorabilia collection, alongside signed copies of pictures of U-M basketball legend and eventual NBA player Cazzie Russell, and U-M baseball star and eventual Detroit Tiger Bill Freehan.

Esch, an army veteran, served five terms in Congress and was a leader of congressional Republicans who urged both President Johnson and President Nixon to end the Vietnam War. He also authored numerous pieces of legislation, including the Comprehensive Employment and Training Act of 1973. Of all the members of the House of Representatives, Congressman Esch was the one asked to represent the House at the funeral of Martin Luther King Jr. He came to talk to my father about the funeral.

But I knew him best from his much more local contact with our family. He and my father liked to talk about current events. I happened to answer the phone the day that a call came in from his Washington, D.C., office to our home: "This is Congressman Esch's office for Rev. Postema on an urgent matter." I was quite impressed that my dad was being consulted in such an emergency. Being the 1960s, it could have been for any of a number of crises. I watched as my dad sat down at the desk and took the phone. My father's first words after listening to Congressman Esch were: "That sounds quite worrisome. Likely needs immediate attention."

Watching carefully, I believed that my father was up to the task of aiding the congressman on any matter; while we lacked tools, my father's study was filled with books on every subject, and he counseled people regularly. My father then gravely repeated something the congressman said: "Yes, complete collapse if not remedied." I became even more concerned about this serious matter that might cause a collapse—perhaps of the country itself. I had a gnawing fear it might be related to those "white objects" in space; they were, perhaps, a threat to the planet. Just the type of thing that had been featured on *Star Trek*.

I watched as my dad sat up, clearly readying himself to take on this burden in aid of the country, rifling for a slip of paper in the desk drawer. "I can get this for you Marv, they will take care of it for you." My father stroked his beard and delivered the evident solution with appropriate conviction in his voice: "Payeur Foundations. Will take good care of this. Here's the number."

My father hung up. "The Esch's house needs some foundation work, and he wanted to know who we had used," he announced. He looked somewhat crestfallen. I think he, too, believed that he was going to be consulted on weightier ethical matters of state.

Later in the year, I was able to discuss the more significant matter weighing on my mind with Congressman Esch, who I knew was also very involved with the space program. I finally told him, when he was back from Washington, that I was quite concerned about the white objects that our neighbor, Mr. Faram, was tracking at Bendix. He seemed intrigued, and like any good politician, he told me that he would most certainly look into that and get back to me.

I was comforted that I was a confidant and had access to insider Washington information.

I was also comforted by the fact that we had neighbors who lent their tools, that my mother had the common sense to put a cop's fingertip in a cool glass of milk, and that my father was an advisor (of sorts) to a congressman.

The next time I saw Congressman Esch, he was again talking to my dad in our front yard, and I asked him again about the white objects. I took his slight hesitation in responding not to mean that he had forgotten about this issue but that this was most likely a highly classified situation that we were discussing. I watched him choose his words carefully. NASA, he assured me, had this situation, whatever it might be, fully under control.

And on Covington Drive that morning, I had no reason to doubt him.

CHAPTER 6
Summer 1967

A Miracle Purchase

BEING OF DUTCH ANCESTRY, I was addicted to a particular type of black licorice from Holland called Dubbel Zout, or double-salted licorice. It was the size of a nickel and had "DZ" imprinted on it. Most people found it horrible, tasting of the presumed taste of battery acid. It also caused your tongue and lips to turn black if you ate too much of it. It was an acquired taste, and we would get a package of this licorice in our Christmas stockings.

This licorice was available at the premier candy venue in town, Drake's Sandwich Shop, right near the Diag on campus. Drake's had a large lunch counter and booths, where students happily ordered sandwiches, grilled pecan rolls, and limeade. But it was the large glass jars of candy that drew me in. I dreamed of this licorice, and other candy, weighed on a large silver scale by the ounce, then packaged in a red-and-white-striped bag. However, early on, without the necessary funds, I did not go to Drake's often.

For those with limited funds, a key place for penny candy was the Blue Front on Packard, near where the great rocker Bob Seger lived for a period of time. My mother saw this shop near campus as a den of iniquity, as the students bought alcohol there, and pornographic magazines were discretely placed, but still visible, in the top shelves above the comic books. Whether the store was virtuous or not, the

Drake's Sandwich Shop. © 1985 MLive Media Group. All Rights Reserved.
Used with permission.

advantage of the Blue Front was that I could always find money on the ground near the entrance.

When I told my mother of the coins we'd find outside the store, it just confirmed her view that some subset of college students wasted money or at least couldn't keep track of it. Perhaps, in her mind, the students were in such a hurry to buy alcohol or pornography that they began pulling the money out of their pockets, spilling loose coins in great anticipation before they even entered the store. "Money must have flown from their pockets," my mother said as she shook her head.

But I liked to go there because of the loose change on the ground and because we almost never had candy in our house. We would get candy from the neighbors on Halloween and carefully parse it out over the subsequent weeks or months. But spending money on candy or other unnecessary things was frowned upon. In our house, frugality was a virtue. So I had to be circumspect when talking about candy or other purchases.

When I had my own funds, I enjoyed going to Delahant's—a store, close to our house, that had candy and comic books and an odd assortment of other goods. It was a store frozen in amber, even in 1967. The windows were tinted, giving the light inside a sepia tint like on old photograph. The air was dusty. The owner had some vision issues but was alert to kids in the store. He preferred that people speak in hushed tones.

One day, I rode my bike up to Delahant's. Just before walking out of the store, I put a coin in a machine near the door. This was no pedestrian gumball machine, rather it dispensed small plastic containers that could be pulled apart and contained dinky plastic toys. The machine was evidently broken, although at that point in time, I simply believed that I had hit the jackpot. The turning mechanism didn't stop, as usual, at one turn, so I kept turning it. After many turns, perhaps twenty-five items came out. I had a bag with me and pushed them all in. I couldn't believe my luck.

Really, a miracle in my view.

When I got home, I made the mistake of putting this collection on the kitchen table to sort rather than taking it immediately to my room. I had done nothing wrong, in my mind, so why not examine the items in public? My parents viewed this acquisition through a different moral lens.

At first, my mother was quite concerned that I had spent significant funds on these cheap plastic toys. This implicated the sin of waste and could likely lead down a path wherein I would become a wastrel, as in the biblical tale of the Prodigal Son. Or a more contemporary fear: a college student wasting money at the Blue Front.

I told her that one nickel had gotten all of this, and I told of my plans to trade these toys with neighbors for other things, including baseball cards. I believed that this explanation would ameliorate the situation. It did not. Upon kind, yet skillful, cross-examination to gather the facts, this situation then became a criminal matter to her, even worse than wasting money.

She believed that this was "just plain stealing," and she spent a significant amount of time gently talking to me about the law and morality, all the while believing that I would see the light and voluntarily offer to take this bounty back.

"We need to discuss this with your father," she said, taking me to my father's study to have him carefully weigh in on this matter with theological implications. Now that we were discussing the matter at this higher level, I raised several counter-arguments and specifically argued the theological defense of miracles.

"This is like the Israelites finding manna from heaven while in the wilderness," I argued. Having been attentive in Sunday school and Vacation Bible School for any and all discussions of miracles, I launched into a further discussion of the peril to those who did not accept such providential miracles.

"O ye of little faith," was not really getting me anywhere.

My father was usually intrigued by theological discussions but had little patience for this discussion of miracles as applied to a broken machine. My mother also found my invocation of theological justifications to be "sputten," a Dutch term for irreverent and flippant, and something to be avoided in our home. Nevertheless, I thought I caught a momentary smile in her eyes for my effort.

My parents were hoping that I would come to a moral awareness about this situation on my own. But, without movement on my part, my father pulled parental rank and simply ordered me into the car, drove up to the store, and brought me in to explain the situation to Mr. Delahant. I turned over the bounty. The most irritating thing about this was that I did not even get a reward for my coerced honesty. My father had assured me that doing the right thing was its own reward.

But this did not seem to be the case at the time.

I gradually but reluctantly accepted this legal and moral framework concerning coin-operated machines. And soon, I found this framework had to be more broadly applied when an issue arose concerning metal slugs (the size and shape of a quarter) found at various building sites.

Word on the street was these slugs would work in the ice-cream sandwich vending machine at the YMCA. This moral dilemma was faced by many kids who went to the YMCA for swim lessons in the 1960s. It apparently was so prevalent that a sign soon was placed on the machine claiming that the use of slugs was a federal crime.

Not wanting to violate federal law, I found that slugs still had value on the open market and could be traded for items and even sold for a couple of pennies to someone who was quite willing to risk federal prosecution for an ice-cream sandwich. The money added up and, in turn, could be used to buy candy—in particular: double-salted black licorice from Drake's, penny candy from the Blue Front, or a variety of items from Delahant's. And many of these purchases were kept out of sight in a shoebox in my closet.

I did not want my mother to worry that I was wasting my money.

CHAPTER 7
Summer 1968

Blowin' in the Wind at
The Ark and on the Diag

IN AUGUST 1968, MY FATHER SHOWED me a picture in *Newsweek* magazine that ran alongside an article on that summer's protests at the Chicago Democratic National Convention. The picture was of a graduate student who attended my dad's student chapel. My dad eventually let him live in a room in the basement of the chapel in exchange for help with the people living on the streets who congregated around the campus. They were often students who had dropped out of college or others whose parents had kicked them out of the house. The street people came from across the state and the country to be in Ann Arbor. I felt some pride that they would come to Ann Arbor. Yet, there was a great deal of pain in their situations.

During the Chicago protest, a policeman had hit this student in the head with a billy club, and as blood poured down his face, a *Newsweek* photographer snapped the picture. I couldn't help but stare at the stitches on the side of his face when I saw him at the chapel. The difficulties of 1968 seemed to distill in the blood and tears in that photo.

There was a palpable malaise in the nation. Rev. Martin Luther King Jr. had talked about it in a speech entitled "A Proper Sense of Priorities" on February 6, 1968, which he gave in Washington, D.C., to a group called Clergy and Laymen Concerned About Vietnam. My

Peace Rally at the Diag in Ann Arbor. © 1969 MLive Media Group. All Rights Reserved. Used with permission.

father had gone to this conference and came back with a reprint of the speech. He read excerpts of it to us at the dinner table: "There is restlessness in the land because the land doesn't seem to have a sense of purpose, a proper sense of policy and a proper sense of priorities."

And the search for purpose in the nation was heightened with the crucial events of 1968. Rev. King was shot and killed two months after my father had seen him speak. Then Bobby Kennedy, who was running for president, was killed two months after that. At the beginning of the school year in the fall, two hundred protestors were arrested on the University campus.

A loud exclamation point to this societal restlessness came when a bomb blast was heard all over Ann Arbor near midnight on September 29, 1968. There was an explosion in an unmarked office that was located on Main Street. This was about a mile from the U-M stadium where President Johnson had given his Great Society speech.

The office was a CIA office that recruited students. In the *Ann Arbor News* that week, the police chief told a local reporter that he suspected the attacks had been planned and carried out by "anti-establishment militants" and that his investigation would focus on "hippies of a college age." I recognized, at the time, that "hippies" covered many people who were roaming the streets of Ann Arbor in 1968, and even those sitting on the lawn of my father's chapel.

In early 1968, members of the White Panther Party, including one of the leaders John Sinclair, moved from Detroit into two large homes on Hill Street, several blocks from my father's chapel. They formed in sympathy with the Black Panther Party and advocated for cultural revolution, legalized marijuana, and other societal changes in a ten-point manifesto in November 1968.

A year after the CIA building bombing, in October of 1969, the government charged a person associated with the White Panthers with conspiracy for the bombing. The suspect was held in prison until July of 1972, when the conspiracy charges were dropped by the government after some legal proceedings. (Years later, I wrote about this legal case as part of a seventh-grade project.)

During these times of turmoil, my father took solace and put energy into a folk music venue and coffee house that was coincidently across the street from the White Panther headquarters on Hill Street. It was called The Ark, and it was a refuge for students to come and listen to music. My father had had a vision for this type of venue at his chapel, but in 1965, he joined with three other local pastors in an effort being planned by First Presbyterian Church. Previously, he had unsuccessfully tried to join with the Episcopalians who had formed another musical venue: Canterbury House. The Presbyterians were evidently a little more accommodating.

My father came home from one of The Ark planning meetings and told the family about it at the dinner table. He told us the possible names. My father had suggested the name "The Ark" from the biblical tale of Noah, as a place of shelter in the storm of the times. Two other names had been considered: The Fish and Oikos, the latter of which means "house" in Greek. We told my dad that no one would want to go to a place called The Fish or named after some Greek word that meant something else. We told him we liked the name The Ark the best. And we were happy to know that the name was adopted by consensus of the newly formed board of directors in December 1965.

We wanted to know what folk music was, and he had us listen to

"Blowin' in the Wind" by Bob Dylan and songs by Pete Seeger, Woody Guthrie, Joan Baez, and others. I became completely obsessed with the many other versions of "Blowin' in the Wind," including Peter, Paul and Mary's, which rose to number two in the *Billboard* Top 100 in 1963. I also began to understand the overlap of folk music and other music when I heard a gospel version of "Blowin' in the Wind" in 1968 by the great singer Sam Cooke, the King of Soul, on the radio.

This song had a similar effect to that of Martin Luther King Jr's eyes looking at me in my father's study. It was a rhetorical call to purpose that was hard to avoid. A cashier at Discount Records knew I liked the song, and would find different versions for me when I went in to look through the bins. My personal favorite was the version by Stevie Wonder, from Detroit, who was only sixteen years old when he recorded it in 1966. The list was endless, including Johnny Cash, Elvis Presley, and Diana Ross & The Supremes. They all sang it. I later even heard Stevie Wonder sing it on TV with Glen Campbell, a country singer. And it kept going. For a song that reportedly was written in ten minutes in April 1962—just a short while before Bob Dylan (spelled Dillon on the poster) came to sing at the Michigan Union Ballroom— the song sure had staying power. It was sorrowful and uplifting, the music adapted from an old spiritual.

My father took us to The Ark, and we listened to all the folk music of the day. Initially, The Ark also held poetry readings, political discussions, and other events. But gradually, the music took over as a balm for the times.

One day in early 1966, just after The Ark had opened, my father came home agitated. He was carrying a copy of *The Michigan Daily* student newspaper and complaining about a recent review of The Ark by a student reporter. The headline "The Ark—Divine Inspiration Lacking" said it all. It continued: "The Ark, a new coffeehouse, is only another two-bit enterprise bound to be beached ... This place has too little and will bomb out."

The reporter then wrote smugly about the no-drug policy: "I didn't mind checking my pot, LSD and glue at the door, but for what? Squirt, orange drink or cola." She must have taken all her drugs before she went into The Ark, as she seemed to have missed the music perfor-

50

mance altogether and claimed that what The Ark needed was live music. There was a folk-rock group that had played that very night, as the manager wrote in a rebuttal.

Despite the review, the founders were even more resolved to support The Ark's mission. And their faith was rewarded. It eventually thrived. Beyond their wildest dreams. And when it was on its way and the churches could no longer support it in the 1970s, it raised its own money. It became one of the premier music venues in the United States. It moved from Hill Street to South Main Street in 1984, then to its current four-hundred-seat venue in the heart of Main Street in downtown Ann Arbor.

While my father was working with others to support a musical place of refuge for the students, I was out and about amongst those same students, attempting to sell items for fundraisers to support my various ventures. Because we lived in a neighborhood with so many children selling the same products door-to-door, the local neighborhood market soon was saturated.

But the University campus provided endless customers, and the University Diag—a large green space, lined with trees and University buildings, with a wide sidewalk diagonally cutting through from two corners—was crucial. The corner of South University and East University was one prime location. The corner of North University and State Street was another. Amid the street preachers, the political activists, the student clubs, and the students walking by, I could be found hawking my wares.

And in the fall of 1968, I could be found selling a small set of miniature screwdrivers, about four inches long, that had different colored handles and came in a nifty compact case. Two dollars. The sale of these screwdrivers would pave my way to Cub Scout camp. One dollar went to cover camp costs. I learned a lot from those on the Diag—the activists, musicians, and others. I tried to position myself near someone strumming a guitar and singing folk music. Just for the effect.

I tried various sales pitches for this set of screwdrivers: How practical this set was. How society would be better if each person had a set. I had limited success with these strategies, but I also watched the signs of other groups, each demanding urgent action for one cause or another. And from this, I found a method that guaranteed success no matter what the product, which I would modify over the years.

My sign: *HELP. NO CAMP. UNLESS. SELL ALL. TODAY.*

I set up between a sorority table recruiting members and a table urging political change, and yes, some folk singers with guitar and bongo drums. "Blowin' in the Wind" was in the air. One person came to talk to me about the camp, gave me a twenty-dollar bill, and didn't even want any screwdrivers. He said, "Keep some for your efforts too." It made little sense to me, but I took the money. And I felt great, as I was able to give away free screwdriver sets to some sorority members, a street preacher, political activists, and just regular students as they walked by. I also kept a set for our family because we had such a poor assortment of tools.

And I must confess that I pocketed some of this money. But not for long; I bought Stevie Wonder's *Blowin' in the Wind* 45 record at Discount Records and then went to Drake's and bought some double-salted black licorice. When I was back selling on the Diag, a potential customer who claimed to be a medical student saw my discolored lips and tongue from the licorice and was worried that I had some rare disease and tried to lure me to the hospital. I showed him the black licorice and gave him a piece. He spit it out.

I had found that my purpose in the fall of 1968 was to explain the virtues of this multicolored kit of screwdrivers—instruments of usefulness to relieve mechanical and other adjustment problems faced by students at the University of Michigan. I was rewarded for my efforts. I sold the most out of anyone in the fundraiser and received a prize: one of the same small screwdriver sets. I brought it to church the next Sunday and gave it to the graduate student who had been hit in the head in Chicago.

He appreciated the gesture.

CHAPTER 8
Fall 1968

———

Home Alone with Jarts

THE WEEK BEFORE THE EXPLOSION rocked the CIA office on Main Street in the fall of 1968, I was nine and my brother was eleven. That was about the age that parents would sometimes leave their kids alone overnight while they went away to visit relatives. And this was not only happening in our household.

We got a Jarts set the weekend before my parents and younger sisters set off to Grand Rapids on a Saturday morning. They would be gone for about thirty-four hours and leave us at home, which seemed fully appropriate at the time. We were, of course, left a list of instructions: chores, homework on Saturday (not on Sunday), limit TV watching (which would prove difficult), stay out of the dilapidated haunted house down the street, and generally stay out of trouble. But that would prove difficult with our new purchase.

What were Jarts? They were roughly eighteen-inch-long plastic darts with a heavy, metal-pointed tip. The point of the game was to throw the Jarts through the air and get them to land in a plastic ring. The plastic rings were placed about forty feet apart, and the object was to get the most in the ring. That was fine, as far as it went. However, there were so many injuries (deaths even) in the 1970s and 1980s that the sale of Jarts was eventually banned. The reason for injury was obvious: what kids most wanted to do was to throw these Jarts wildly

53

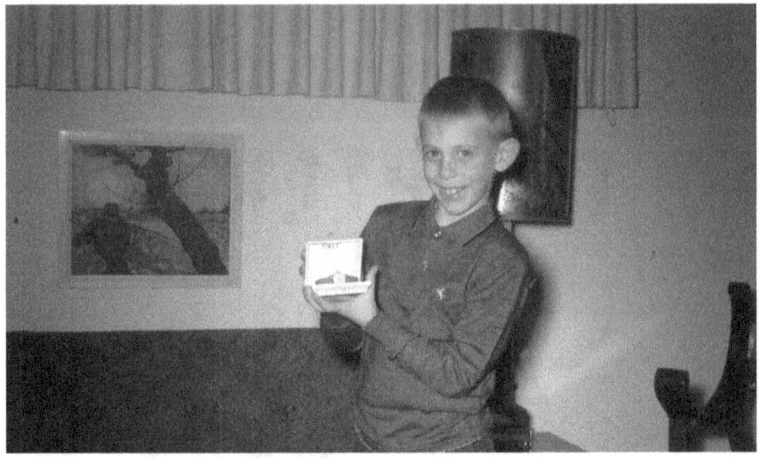

Me with a new watch so I can time things.

and as high as possible and see the result.

Our game that Saturday afternoon (after a favorite cartoon called *Jonny Quest*) disintegrated into just that. At one point, both of the Jarts landed on the roof of our neighbor Officer Fleming's house, hit some metal flashing, and bounced around in a manner that would have sounded like gunfire to someone knowledgeable. Needless to say, Officer Fleming came out of his house, pistol drawn. Reflexively, learned from watching TV, my brother and I both put our hands in the air.

Officer Fleming watched over our neighborhood and the Postema family in particular. We told him what had happened, and we proceeded to get a ladder and retrieve our weapons of mass disruption. He knew our parents were gone for the weekend. He instructed us to put the Jarts back in the shed and said that we should go inside and watch television for the entire rest of the day (or that's what we heard at least). This directive from a sworn police officer was a command that, to us, superseded any instruction from the parents about television moderation.

While we were getting such advice, I casually asked him about homework on Sundays, which he thought was a good idea also. We took this as a command to delay doing any further homework until Sunday, and along with his other directive, we began watching television as soon as possible. The nighttime TV watching began fittingly with a cop show. We then ventured into the weird zone of Channel 9, the Canadian Broadcasting Corporation, and got into some late-night horror movies. Somewhat freaked out by then, we brought the Jarts in from the shed and placed one near each door to be used as weapons to fend off any nocturnal dangers.

It was, in fact, a restless night, although we did not have to use the Jarts further. We had to be up early, as our parents had arranged for neighbors to drive us to Sunday school and church, followed by a heavy Sunday-noon dinner. We had a tough time making it through all of this due to the lack of sleep.

Nevertheless, we had a good afternoon listening to the recent Beatles hit "Hey Jude," among others on the radio, as we worked side by side on our homework. We also discussed the fortunes of the Detroit Tigers, who seemed to be doing well—and would, in fact, win the World Series the next month. Turning off the radio, we completed our memory homework, which involved reciting long passages to each other and correcting them as necessary. We would be called upon on Monday morning to recite them in school (and would be graded on this). Having completed this task, we were both feeling better.

Our parents pulled into the driveway just as we finished our homework. My mom was quite pleased that we had evidently done very well on our own, although ever observant about the state of affairs in the house, she did want to know more about why the Jarts stood by the doors like guards.

CHAPTER 9
1969-1970

Sabbatical Year

THE DETAILS OF THE TRIP WERE leaked slowly to us in the spring of 1969. We knew we were going to drive in our old blue station wagon over the summer to Berkeley, California, where my father would take a year's sabbatical. His work as a student pastor in the center of the U-M campus in 1968 had not been easy.

More details came trickling in. We would travel the whole way, pulling a pop-up trailer that would sleep the six of us. We would camp, and my mom would feed us from a one-burner stove on the way. Where we would actually stay in Cuernavaca, Mexico—our destination for a monthlong detour to attend a conference—or where we would live in Berkeley were details not shared with us. But this seemed to be part of a hushed series of discussions between my parents.

The Postema kids were ages eleven, ten, seven, and four, and we were intrigued by this trip and its accompanied lack of specifics. My serious older brother had maps and wanted additional information. My father said we were going to remain flexible. My mother began to plan the practical details of the trip. The car and the camper were going to hold all of the things we would need to live for nine months in Berkeley. Food was to be stored in a green Coleman cooler that would need ice.

My stuff went in a Strohs Beer carton. In it, I fit a small amount

Camping in Santa Fe, New Mexico, August 1969.

of clothing; an extra pair of shoes; a guidebook on improving basket-ball skills; a red Harris stamp-collection binder; a white plastic Argus camera; a notebook and some pens; and the "C" volume of the 1945 edition of the red World Book Encyclopedia, containing a summary and maps of California. I also took all the money I had.

In Cuernavaca, Mexico, we ended up staying on the grounds of a Catholic girls' boarding school, where the conference took place. The school was a Garden of Eden with a kidney-shaped pool. We set up the camper and were given the key to an eleventh-grade classroom, containing various textbooks, and importantly, a bathroom and sink.

We had no supervision during the day, and we roamed around, caught small iguanas and let them go, and went into the city to play soccer in the city square. Over the month we were there, more items ended up in the beer box: a Mexican poncho vest, sandals made of straw and tires, a silver peace-sign ring, a twenty-five-peso commem-orative coin from the 1968 Mexico City Olympics, some Mexican stamps for my collection, and a bullhorn from a bullfight we went to.

My father listened all day to famous theologians and philosophers, such as Ivan Illich. In the evening, we listened to Mexican music and drank ice-cold Squirt and Coke out of small bottles. Later at night, popular folk songs serenaded us as we fell asleep: "Where Have All the Flowers Gone?," "This Land Is Your Land," "Leaving on a Jet Plane," and "Four Strong Winds."

Getting into Mexico was much easier than getting back into the United States. What possessed the federal agents to decide to carefully examine our station wagon and trailer on that ninety-five-degree day was a mystery. They tapped the wood paneling on the station wagon and looked under the car. My father had told them he was a minister coming back from a conference, but this held no sway; the agents were perhaps the type of atheists I had been warned about in parochial school: those who persecuted the clergy. Or they had looked at my bearded father and our loaded-down station wagon and came to certain conclusions.

We had to sit on a bench while they opened the trailer and removed all the boxes, and even the green cooler. They took them out and dumped the contents on the table. One agent even looked inside my stamp album. I breached protocol and asked if I could have my "C" volume of the encyclopedia while we waited. The agent said no, and then, adding insult to injury, leafed carefully through it himself.

Having our car and camper searched in front of the family humiliated my mother. She began to realize that the United States agents thought her family members were drug dealers. She didn't even have to say it; I knew exactly what she was thinking: "We are United States citizens from Ann Arbor Michigan. We live next to a U.S. Congressman. My son is being deprived of his reading material."

My mother remained stoic. But once we were released from custody, she made it quite clear to my father that she would not be cooking Dinty Moore stew or Kraft mac and cheese or anything else that night in "a treeless, sweltering KOA campground in Laredo, Texas."

The closest I had ever heard my mother get to swearing was the term "God-forsaken place," and she used it that day. My father, who took issue with the idea that any place in the world was God-forsaken, read the situation correctly, having taken many pastoral psychology classes. We stayed that night in a cheap motel with a big pool and a drive-in hamburger place nearby.

Having been in the seven-foot by eight-foot by five-foot camper for well over a month, this motel room with air-conditioning seemed palatial. Everyone took very long hot showers. We then drank cold vanilla shakes. And we were happy that night in Laredo, Texas.

Despite this rough reentry, we eventually made it to California after a meandering trip through New Mexico, Colorado, and Arizona. The final stages of the trip eventually tested our family harmony. The only direct casualty was a four-inch red-haired troll doll. Without warning, my father snatched it and threw it out of the car window with one hand, and it disappeared into the canyon; his other hand remained firmly on the steering wheel. I was impressed by his decisiveness. This action resolved an ownership dispute that had raged for twenty miles.

When we made it to Berkeley, we found out that my father had not yet arranged for a house for us to live in. As we pulled into a parking space by the Berkeley campus for the first time, a procession of protesting women who were without shirts or bras passed us while carrying signs. My younger sister pointed.

Without blinking an eye, my mom explained that we were in a new place now, and evidently, sometimes the women did not wear shirts. "Things might be different here, but it is not polite to stare," she said, adding, "Remember where we are from. Michigan. And we have good manners."

We all got out of the car and surveyed the Berkeley campus. I was wearing my newly purchased Mexican poncho over a University of Michigan t-shirt, along with Mexican sandals and long athletic socks.

While my family started walking ahead, I lingered by the car, taking in the scene.

"Cool poncho," a young man with very long hair said as he approached.

Looking at the camper, he asked, "Would your family be interested in joining a new family commune?"

"I don't think so, the camper works pretty well," I said, although I didn't know what a commune was.

CHAPTER 10
Spring 1970

Earwigs, Stamps, and Protests

MY PARENTS FOUND A HOUSE in Richmond. It was about eight miles from the Berkeley campus, down San Pablo Avenue, a busy street. The house was unfurnished, so we relied on the kindness of strangers for furniture donations. My father preached at a church as a guest pastor, and he described our trip out there. A good thing about church folk is that they are generous. Some furniture suddenly arrived, including a previously used metal bed, with holes in the frame for restraints, from the local psychiatric hospital. I got to have this bed.

Having settled into the house and beginning to get comfortable in California, I continued to follow the news of the Zodiac Killer on the loose in the Bay Area. The papers had published a cryptogram that the serial killer claimed contained his identity. I spent much of the year trying to decipher the cryptogram, convinced that I somehow would be able to do this when the police were not.

And I settled into my second new living situation; I particularly liked that opportunities for extra credit were abundant in the California public school I attended. For example, I even got extra credit for bringing my stamp collection in to class one day to show a range of three-cent stamps celebrating various states. One of my classmates asked about the two empty stamp squares in my album. I told him I was saving money for these two, one of Thomas Jefferson and one of George Washington. He told me of a stamp store in Berkeley that would likely have them.

Visiting the store, located near the Berkeley University campus, proved fortuitous. They had the stamps. But they were expensive. However, on that visit, I saw a sign on a kiosk that said a company was seeking individuals to collect live earwigs for a scientific research company—fifty cents for a dozen. The company was in Richmond. My mind raced. A small brownish bug with abdominal pincers: a source of income and likely an opportunity for some sort of extra credit project.

My brother was all in. A quick estimate told us that ten thousand earwigs would yield $450—$225 for each of us. This would, of course, mean that we would need to capture about one thousand earwigs per month for ten months. This seemed doable. My brother had read that they liked to inhabit wet corrugated cardboard, so we each went to the grocery store, found and ripped up boxes, and moistened them. We then placed them out in a huge fenced canyon area in the back of the house, past the property line, that had a *"Warning No Trespassing"* sign. *"Possible Electrocution."* It was a secure area for electric lines.

It was also the perfect place for the cardboard, as the sign ensured that we would be undisturbed by others in our venture and no one would take our cardboard. It was slow at first, but every couple of weeks, we delivered the earwigs to the company located in a sketchy area of Richmond. We did not reach our goal, but we brought in around five thousand earwigs by April. Over a hundred dollars each.

One day in May, I crammed all of this money—both bills and a large amount of change—into my pockets. I had planned this day carefully. I would ride a bike into Berkeley, get the stamps, and on the way back, treat myself to lunch at an H. Salt Esq. Fish & Chips. I told my mom I was going to hang out with friends for the day because she had heard rumored protests over the Kent State shootings and warned me about getting anywhere near campus. I didn't want her to be worried about me. I felt justified because I had been planning to get these two stamps for some time. My pants sagged with the weight of my money.

It took a while to get down San Pablo Ave. As I got closer to the campus, I heard sirens and smelled smoke. There was yelling and chanting. There were large groups of students with protest signs. Police

South University Riot, June 1969. My mother hoped that Berkeley, CA, in 1970 would be more peaceful. Image from "Doug Fulton Collection." Used with permission.

were in riot gear. A cop tried to turn me around. "Just going to the stamp store," I said, like it was a normal day. When I finally got to the stamp and coin shop, it was boarded up.

Dispirited, I turned back and decided to salvage the day with the planned fish and chips. The riot was still in progress, and I got off my bike to find a better route. "Do you have any money?" a protestor menacingly said as he put down his peace protest sign.

"Yes, I have lots of money," I replied, "for expensive stamps." My lack of street savvy attracted the attention of some of his friends, including one in Hare Krishna clothing.

It happened fast, and I got humiliated. I was held upside down by my feet as they emptied my pockets, just like in a cartoon. I was in a fury but couldn't land any blows. I suppose it could have been worse. They took all of my money and threw me into the bushes. They left me with little dignity but did not take my bicycle. And, a detail that would puzzle me for some time, they took only one of my shoes.

I immediately approached another police officer, who was none too happy I was engaging him; he was behind a riot shield. "I'm from Michigan." The policeman seemed furious at me for being there at all.

My anger at the situation propelled me home as I stewed over the details. The fact that this was at a peace march? With someone posing as a peaceful Hare Krishna? It was too much. Also, what was I going to tell my mother about the money and the shoe? This was clearly my punishment for lying to her in the first place.

As I passed a shoe store, I actually stopped and seriously contemplated stealing only one shoe from it. But this might make things worse. The shoes wouldn't match. I then thought it might be easier to steal a pair. I felt ashamed that these criminal thoughts were overtaking me. I stayed for a while, looking at the store and contemplating criminal acts. But I finally decided it wasn't worth it.

As I rode home, eventually, the words of the recent Simon & Garfunkel hit "Bridge Over Troubled Water" offered comfort as I hummed the tune.

I then met some friends, and they walked me home. Of course, the first thing my mom said when I walked in was "Where is your shoe?" It all came out. The stamps. The riots. The robbery. The lack of police protection. My lack of a lunch of fish and chips.

We would talk about this further when my father got home. It turned out, he was at the riots too. He was sympathetic to the concerns of the students but very wisely had worn his clerical collar.

We left a wild year in California to go back to Ann Arbor before the school year ended. My mother decided that she needed to see her father immediately because he had fallen ill. She was going to fly to Pella, Iowa, with my sisters. My father, brother, and I would make the trek home in the camper.

I felt she must have had great devotion to my grandfather to forgo the great opportunity to camp across the United States for a second time in the small camper, our clothes in beer boxes, our one-burner stove in tow. By the time we arrived in Iowa, my grandfather was fine.

I assumed my mother's mere presence had hastened his recovery.

CHAPTER 11
1970-1971

St. Paul Lutheran School and "Let It Be"

WHEN WE ARRIVED BACK IN ANN ARBOR in the summer of 1970, I had a lot of catching up to do. I had to rejoin my Little League baseball team—sponsored by Weber's Inn—for another run at last place. I enrolled in Pioneer High School's Basketball School for the summer. I went to the library and renewed my membership card. I reclaimed all of my lawn-mowing clients and got some new ones. And I expanded into a new venture: a three-hundred-house paper route for a weekly paper, the *Huron Valley Ad-Visor*. I was getting back into the routine of Ann Arbor.

I also needed money. Primarily for a stereo, a new bike, and records.

Despite the return to familiar surroundings, as I started sixth grade back in Ann Arbor, I knew I had changed. I wore a silver peace ring from Mexico. I owned two pairs of bell-bottom pants. I had grown my hair out over the past year. My sister had made me a bracelet of colored "love beads" purchased from the Middle Earth store down on campus.

And I had seen many things on the way to California and back. The lyrics to Steppenwolf's "Born to Be Wild" resonated with me, talking about heading out on the road and looking for adventure.

I was just like Peter Fonda and his friends in the movie *Easy Rider*, except I wasn't on a motorcycle; I was being driven by my father, with my family, in an old station wagon.

I had been transformed by the trip in many ways. I had haggled in the markets of Mexico and been to a bullfight. I had seen the beauty of numerous state parks and national parks throughout the country. I had surreptitiously bought a very large hunting knife in Colorado. I had witnessed student protests firsthand. And I had successfully avoided the Zodiac serial killer. For an entire year.

In addition, I had been to the famous Glide Memorial Church in San Francisco and seen the great preacher and civil rights activist Cecil Williams preach so powerfully that I thought I had heard God himself. (Sidenote: the collection that Sunday had been for a breakfast program in Oakland run by the Black Panther Party.) I had also gone to Grace Cathedral, the Episcopal cathedral on the top of Nob Hill, to hear Duke Ellington and his orchestra play.

Now, back in Michigan, I became recognized among my friends as an expert on the state of California. I could talk about the Pacific Ocean, Yosemite National Park, the Redwood forests, and Disneyland. I also extolled the virtues of my new favorite food: fish and chips.

Ann Arbor had changed while I was gone; it had not waited for the Postema family to return, and it too had experienced its share of protests and concern about many aspects of the state of the nation. The campus held a Vietnam moratorium in October 1969. Then, in April 1970, the University's four-day "Teach-In on the Environment" for Earth Day at Crisler Arena was a huge success and had a long-term impact. The college students were restless, and change was in the air. On March 19, 1970, over eight hundred marchers protested their dissatisfaction with the university's position on minority enrollment. The rally was called by the Black Action Movement (BAM).

Despite all this going on, however, St. Paul Lutheran School had not changed much. I had been together with sixteen of my classmates since first grade. Written in 1529, Martin Luther's "*Luther's Small Catechism*," which we diligently worked through each year, was exactly the same in form and content. We were required to memorize large passages from the catechism or Bible verses and recite them each week for a grade. (I confess that the competitive aspect of memory work, rather than any spiritual aspect, greatly appealed to me.)

Hot lunch was also the same. It was served mainly by German women volunteers, in white uniforms and hairnets, from the Lutheran

St. Paul Lutheran School, 1965. Image used with permission of St. Paul School of Ann Arbor.

Church. Make no mistake, there were some very good things about that, such as pigs in a blanket and spatzen noodles, or bratwurst and fried potatoes. But each lunch also contained at least one helping of sauerkraut or red cabbage or coleslaw or beets. (To this day, I cannot bear to even look at any of these.)

The principal of the school, also my sixth-grade teacher, Mr. Richert, had not changed. With short hair and a nondescript dark suit, he might have come from any recent decade. Despite some additional cultural run-ins with him, primarily about long hair, he actually gave me a lot of slack. He allowed me to leave class and work as an aide in the library, returning to a job I had done in second grade. He gave me extra math projects to do and also put me to work tutoring other students in the subject. He encouraged my efforts in basketball and got me running track. As the principal, he had to leave the class at times to deal with some crisis, so he sometimes left the class alone with projects to complete and asked me to keep an eye on things. My desk remained right next to his the whole year.

Every day started with devotions led by a member of the class. A student had to read a Bible verse and talk about it. Maybe pick out a hymn. Do *something*. I felt the need to change the dynamics of this devotional time. So I began with music.

I carefully prepared my pitch, and I reminded Mr. Richert what we had been taught every year: Martin Luther believed that music was a divine gift and even capable of promoting good and fighting evil. Luther saw music as comfort to people in times of personal struggle. And Luther loved young people and dabbled with secular music himself.

So, as a test run, I chose for my devotions "Oh Happy Day" by The Edwin Hawkins Singers, which I had heard at Glide Memorial Church in San Francisco. This song had risen to number four on the *Billboard* Hot 100 in 1969. Its optimism and gospel beat went over pretty well with my classmates. Another student followed suit and brought in the popular new rendition of the hymn "Amazing Grace" by Judy Collins. My father was quite happy that this was being played by popular music stations. (And this was not an isolated event, given the interconnections of music: Elvis Presley, Sam Cooke, Willie Nelson, Aretha Franklin, Al Green, Ray Charles, and Johnny Cash all put out versions of "Amazing Grace" in the 1960s and 1970s.)

Then I began to descend a slippery slope. I brought in one of the top songs of 1970, The Beatles' "Let It Be," and I explained to Mr. Richert that my father had confirmed that the phrase "let it be" was really a rough translation of the word "amen." Mr. Richert respected my father, and he let the song go through. I could see it was testing his patience, though, when I noticed the muscles in his temples twitch. After that, he put a pause in modern music for a while.

But when George Harrison's "My Sweet Lord" hit the top of the music charts in late 1970 and early 1971, it was too much to resist. I convinced my friend that he should bring it in for devotions. But I cautioned him to stop the record before it got to the "Hare Krishna" part. The song was written to honor the Hindu God Krishna, but it took a while to get to that point. My friend agreed but then forgot to stop the song. As the Hare Krishna refrain kicked in, everyone smiled—except for Mr. Richert. He pulled the plug on this song, and popular music was curtailed.

But only for a while.

An opportunity arose to protest his unilateral decision. One day, we were told we were having a substitute teacher the next day and that she was hard of hearing, so we would need to speak up. I was assigned devotions that day. The sub was unaware of the music prohibition. I told her I was going to play "Joy to the World" as part of my presentation. She said fine, although she mentioned that the Christmas season had passed. I told her it was a newer version that was currently the number one hit in the United States. And it was.

Three Dog Night's "Joy to the World." The beats started echoing from the walls, then the story of their friend Jeremiah the Bullfrog blasted through the room.

And as the class was enjoying the song, I watched as concern spread on the sub's face. Afterwards, she asked me, "Did I hear something about sweet love?" I assured that she had not heard correctly, that the words were "make sweet wine for you"—the parable of turning water into wine of course.

She said she also heard something about loving the ladies. I explained that this actually was "I love the laities." I added that Three Dog Night was quite likely a Lutheran group itself. This was clear because the phrase fit right in with Lutheran doctrine, as Martin Luther loved the laity (the common people of the church) and wanted to abolish the distinction between clergy and the laity.

And I just kept going in my explanation: This love of the laities, in fact, brought about the Protestant Reformation. "Martin Luther was a radical," I reminded her and the class. She nodded along with all of this, but I don't think she could hear anything I was saying.

Class discussion about the song went on for some time. She even let me play it again at the end of the day. And I opened the classroom door for everyone to hear it in the hallways. And, to her credit—or because of her hearing issues—the sub evidently never ratted on me to Mr. Richert.

I went home from school humming Three Dog Night to myself, thinking about the joy and boys and girls and fishes and deep blue sea.

I knew then that I was ready to move on from St. Paul elementary, but I had to admit that I was grateful for all I had learned there and the sheer goodness of that day.

The smiles of the class when I explained the Lutheran lyrics to the sub, something interesting in math, the best lunch possible (fish sticks, french fries, and applesauce). And the library, dodgeball during gym, and random conversations. Finally, beating the huge bass drum with unbridled enthusiasm and as loud as I could during band class.

The substitute teacher that day had brought the boys and girls together in the deep blue sea of sixth grade and let us do what we wanted.

That song was a reflection of the joy in my world that day.

CHAPTER 12
Fall 1970

The Treasure Mart

IN THE FALL OF 1970, my brother and I needed a stereo very badly. We were playing 45 rpm records on a very old red 45 player. It was slightly off, making the music of the day slowed down and oddly distorted. This could not go on.

We knew what to do. Our house was filled with used furniture obtained from classified ads, garage sales, and most importantly, a thrift store on Detroit Street. Detroit Street was paved in brick, just as it was when the building that housed the thrift store was built in 1869.

The classifieds were good for a focused purchase, such as when my mom snagged a set of bunk beds for my sisters, which were purchased from former Detroit Mayor Jerome Cavanagh, who had recently moved to Ann Arbor. A purchase like this would come with a belief that the bed needed to be treated with particular respect.

Garage sales were iffy, as one could never predict when they would happen.

But the thrift store, the Treasure Mart, was always reliable. Its large and steady flow of used goods never ceased. Originally a steam-powered planing mill, the building was the site of many more businesses before it became the iconic blue Treasure Mart in 1960.

The main floor had the best stuff. Large dining-room tables packed precariously with china, clocks, candlestick holders, lamps, and silver-

Treasure Mart, 1978. © Susan Wineberg, Creative Commons (Attribution, Non-Commercial, Share-alike), aadl.org/node/573427.

ware—so covered that the wood of the table was barely visible. One hard bump against any of the many tables could send things flying. Glass cabinets cradled an enchanting world of jewelry and other valuable items. The store was always filled to capacity with both goods and shoppers. Treasure Mart made people happy.

My mother would visit regularly, looking for a bargain, a gem hidden in the clutter that would be perfect somewhere in our house. We loved to go with her and watch her search and make calculations about the goods. We sometimes would tease our youngest sister—who was smaller and darker haired than her tall, blond siblings—and say that we actually got her at the Treasure Mart. She was thrilled to get this news, as it meant she was special.

The other thing that made the Treasure Mart a favorite was the risk analysis involved in purchasing items. When a new item came in, it received a set price, but the longer it sat in the store, the more the price would be reduced—sometimes as much as 10 percent a week depending on the item. This policy moved the merchandise. Each person had to decide if they would purchase early for a higher price or wait and risk losing it.

People shifted their risk analysis each week, as well as their calculations of happiness. People went in each day with their hopes and cash, picking up objects of desire and perhaps placing them back in a somewhat less visible place, where they would check for them in a week. Nothing stayed in place long. Everything was a bet.

Our family often bet on the reductions.

Sometimes, we lost.

But oftentimes, my mom had timed it just right.

So, my brother and I were prepared to go to the Treasure Mart to find the stereo that we needed to get us through the 1970s. We efficiently went through the floors of the Treasure Mart and were rewarded for our effort. There sat a Lloyd's stereo set, priced at ninety dollars but due for a reduction soon. We needed that discount. We moved the stereo back to the corner of the room near the electrical outlet to check out the radio on it. It sounded good. And while we had not intended this, we suddenly realized that it was now very hard to spot the stereo back in this corner.

We didn't consider this to be in any way unethical. Still, we realized that this might prove to be a tactical advantage. So we left it there.

When we came back two weeks later, it was gone.

Or so it seemed. Upon closer inspection, someone had carefully put a very unattractive carpet remnant over the stereo. Moreover, the carpet remnant was somewhat grimy and not something anyone would want to touch. In desperation, we pulled it back to find the stereo, and we were relieved that it was still there. We calculated that the price would now likely be around seventy-two dollars, which fit our budget.

We discussed how unethical the actions of our unknown stereo-buying adversary had been. But I really had to hand it to them, as it had been very carefully camouflaged; the filthy carpet was an ingenious touch. It was hard not to begin thinking of all sorts of related schemes to hide merchandise in the store. The entire store was suddenly a veritable terrain of hiding places and possible subterfuge.

Meanwhile, as we were standing with the carpet pulled back, a salesclerk came by and came down hard on us for attempting to hide the stereo. "That is a disgusting carpet," she added.

We protested our innocence. "This was not us," we explained, "we found it this way!"

She looked skeptical. "Our father's a pastor," I said to aid the

STEPHEN POSTEMA

cause. She seemed unmoved.

My brother and I decided we had to act now lest other buyers swoop in. The clerk said she might have to mark it up since it likely had been hidden for a while.

"This would not be fair," I argued and pulled out the seventy-five dollars we had. We told her about our old 45 player.

"We are missing out on all the good albums," I said. I told her that we were going to go to Discount Records and buy our first album, *Bridge Over Troubled Water* by Simon & Garfunkel, released earlier that year. This seemed to soften her.

"Good choice," she said.

We picked up the stereo and went to the cash register to close the deal. The salesclerk, perhaps in an attempt to walk back the accusatory initial interaction, suggested that we look in the fifty-cent record album bin, as they had gotten some new ones in. She said that, under the circumstances, I could have four for a dollar, but there was no guarantee they weren't scratched. I wasn't sure what circumstances she was referring to: being falsely accused of hiding the stereo, or missing an entire decade of albums.

Either way, I now had the perfect opportunity. I looked through the bin and found an old Stevie Wonder album, *Up-Tight,* which had "Blowin' in the Wind" on it. I also found *Lady Soul* by Aretha Franklin and James Taylor's *Sweet Baby James*, with its blue cover.

Finally, I nabbed the recently released *Hey Jude* album by The Beatles, with The Beatles standing in a doorway on the cover. In the right-hand corner of that album was a handwritten note in red pen that said, "Happy Birthday Ben, I love you as much as The Beatles, Julia." I didn't think much about how this album had made it into the bin—it was now mine, along with the other three.

After we got home with the stereo, we went to Discount Records to purchase *Bridge Over Troubled Water*. We played it repeatedly, along with the four other albums. We ranked the songs, and we deciphered the meaning of the words as best as we could. And we plotted further album purchases.

We had good speakers to hear the music of the decades.

Life could not be better.

CHAPTER 13
Spring 1971

Middle Earth and the Peace-Sign Necklace

ONE SATURDAY IN MAY 1971, I was on a particular mission to buy a silver peace-sign necklace. I was in Middle Earth on South University, in the heart of the campus. I looked carefully at the young woman with wire-rimmed glasses behind the counter. She had frizzy hair, wore a macramé belt, large hoop earrings, a choker-style necklace, and a t-shirt with the word "REVOLT" overlaying a picture of a clenched fist. She looked a little like the Janis Joplin picture next to the cash register. This store clerk looked like she would be just the right person to help me.

Middle Earth sold everything that countercultural students could want: a wide range of drug paraphernalia, political buttons, books, beads, cards, candles, and jewelry. The strong smell of incense made my head pound. Because of the open display of drug items, it felt vaguely criminal to even be in the store. But it was also so psychedelic and cool, and I liked to peruse the large selection of black light posters.

"You know who she is?" the store clerk asked while I was looking at the picture of Janis Joplin.

"Of course," I said, "everyone does, she died last year."

The woman said she had heard Joplin two years ago when the singer had come to Ann Arbor to perform at Crisler Arena.

"Did she play 'Piece of My Heart'?" I asked. She inquired about how I knew the song and whether I knew that Joplin went by the nickname "Pearl." I nodded.

"A person over at Discount Records told me about both," I explained.

Middle Earth had a lot of peace-sign necklaces, so she had even more questions for me. "No, it is not for my sister," I told her. It was for a classmate who sat next to me in the back of the class. It was a graduation present; we would be going to different junior high schools next year. The clerk asked what sort of statement I wanted to make. I said I just thought she would like one.

She then pressed me on a number of things that were personal, but for some reason, I didn't mind telling her. And then she repeated back what I had said to her in an official sounding way:

"So, you go to a church school. You pass notes to each other in the back row of class ... Okay ... And you talk to each other, sometimes about math. She sits very straight in her chair ... Alright now ... She laughed at some con you played on a substitute teacher last week. And she likes the peace-sign ring you wear that you got in Mexico."

"Hell yes, makes perfect sense to me about you getting her this necklace," she concluded.

And when she summarized it like this, with a swear word thrown in, it was clear to me that I was doing the right thing. While I looked very carefully at the selections, I told her to pick out a necklace that she thought would be best. I told her I had the money because I had four jobs. She found the silver peace-sign necklace that she thought would be best. Before I left, the young woman provided a colorful box for it.

She said that she would give me a partial discount since I had a good cause.

While biking home, I debated whether to show it to my mom. I decided that she would think it was a nice gesture, so I did. My mother examined it closely, unfortunately with the price tag still on it. She immediately expressed concern that it was too extravagant a gift. She patiently explained that this was the type of gift you would give someone when you were a lot older. And having been born in the Depression, my mom just shook her head at the price. Less patiently, I explained that this was my money and I could do whatever I wanted with it.

Middle Earth & Vaudeville Delicatessen, November 1975 © Ann Arbor District Library, Creative Commons (Attribution, Non-Commercial, Share-alike), aadl.org/node/636515.

"Hard earned money," I reminded her: paper route, lawn mowing business, snow shoveling, and janitorial work. And then what I thought would be the clincher, "I got a discount." My mom remained resolute.

She recommended that I go back to the store and "reconsider things." So, to appease my mom, I went back to Middle Earth and bought a much cheaper black light poster. I saw the same salesclerk and told her I was going to give my classmate the poster. I let her know what had happened with my mom and what I planned to do about it.

She looked at me and smiled, "Subversive." Then added, "You have to do what you have to do," the clenched fist on her shirt giving her an air of authority.

As I was leaving, she casually asked whether I was considering stealing the book placed by the door. It was student radical Abbie Hoffman's new book, famously titled *Steal This Book*. She said she didn't care if I did; the store had budgeted for thefts of it.

I was already planning to engage in the sin of omission upon my return home, a sin of commission—the theft of a book—was a little too much for me that same afternoon. I told her that, honestly, I wouldn't want to steal a book that I didn't have time to read. It wouldn't be very respectful. And I had limited time. Sixth grade and my jobs were proving to be a lot of work.

"Peace," she said as I walked out of the incensed air of Middle Earth into the fresh air.

When I showed the black light poster to my mom, my brother laughed. "Do you know if she even has a black light?" he asked. I had to admit that I hadn't considered this. My mom thought it was an appropriate gift. But importantly, my mom never asked further about the necklace.

And it was still in the box in my pocket.

The lesson I learned that day was that it was important, at times, to provide only a certain amount of information to parents. Limited information was really in their best interest, I reasoned. I also reminded myself that my mother often said herself, "Sometimes, it is best to say nothing at all."

I certainly thought this was one of those times.

Finally, I rationalized that my mom had only asked me to "reconsider things," and I had certainly done that. Upon reconsideration in Middle Earth that afternoon, I thought it best to let my mom feel good about the black light poster gift and her parental advice. And on further consideration, it was equally important to not have her worry about the necklace gift any longer.

In any event, I had other things to plan for.

My parents let me invite six friends to a postponed birthday/graduation party at Bimbo's pizza parlor downtown. A popular spot that had a Dixieland band, shelled peanuts, and unlimited amounts of Faygo Red Pop, Bimbo's was possibly the furthest thing conceptually from Middle Earth. I invited five of my longtime friends and the classmate to whom I had given both the black light poster and peace-sign necklace.

I was drinking Red Pop when she strolled into Bimbo's wearing a white dress with a red bow. When I saw that she was wearing the necklace, I snorted the Red Pop through my nose in an unsightly way. As I was trying to control this, I stood up and started to slip on the peanut shells on the floor. I gripped the edge of the table to steady myself, feeling the peanut shell residue beneath my fingers. While trying to wipe the red nasal liquid off my best shirt, I waved to her with a hand that now was covered with an unholy mixture of pop, snot, and peanut grime.

The girl came over to sit between my mom and me. When she saw my hand, as I had raised it to whisper to her, she moved even closer to my mom. I was trying to whisper to her to not tell my mom that I had given her the necklace. But with the Dixieland band playing loudly, she evidently thought I had asked her to do the opposite. So, I heard her telling my mom all about the necklace and the black light poster. They just chatted away in detail about it as we ate pizza.

After the party, and after dropping her and another friend off, I waited for my mom to say something. But nothing. Nothing, *all* the way down Main Street, to the unlit Scio Church Road, to home. At home, I looked right at her and thanked her for the party. She smiled and said she enjoyed talking with my friends. She said nothing about the necklace or the act of omission I had committed. For my twelfth birthday, my mom let it slide.

Just let it slide.

The next time I was in Middle Earth, I told the clerk about the party, the Red Pop, my hand, the girl walking in with her necklace, and my mom's grace. She laughed.

"Crazy," she said.

And she pointed at the picture of Janis Joplin on the counter, touched me on the arm, and laughingly proclaimed, "I'm telling you— Pearl would have gotten a real kick out of all this."

CHAPTER 14
Summer 1971

Drum Set

I TOLD THE CLERK AT DISCOUNT RECORDS that I had been playing the drums in the sixth grade and could even take the snare drum home on the weekends to practice. He recommended that I listen to the drums on "Wipe Out" by The Surfaris. Upon hearing it, I had to have a drum set as soon as possible. As I walked my weekly paper route, making money for my own drum set, I would stop and listen to drums being played in other basements all over our neighborhood.

When I had earned enough money for the purchase, I began scanning the "Musical Instruments" section of the *Ann Arbor News* classifieds for one. I was on my own in this venture, as my parents had made it clear that their budget for musical instruments and instruction did not include funds for a drum set.

It turned out that my parents eventually had money for a flute for my sister and a viola for my other sister. They also found the funds for Interlochen Arts Academy for both of the girls over time and were able to send my brother to South America on a choral singing tour with Youth for Understanding. Yet, money for a drum set was not forthcoming.

But while the inequity in musical funding was a topic of discussion amongst my siblings for decades, I understood the basic point: With the allocation of scarce resources, my siblings simply had more musical

Discount Records, 1970. © Ann Arbor District Library, Creative Commons (Attribution, Non-Commercial, Share-alike), aadl.org/node/260095.

ability than I did—a fact that I had to readily admit. Just listening to them play or sing reinforced this point to me.

Furthermore, whether I would stick with drumming was also a legitimate concern. We all started with half-hour piano lessons at the U-M music school, but I didn't last very long. Frankly, I found it hard to sit still for the lessons or to practice regularly, so I abandoned the piano.

But lack of financial support did not dampen my enthusiasm for percussion. And eventually, with two crisp one-hundred-dollar bills in my pocket, my dad drove me to an apartment near campus to look at a pearl grey Ludwig drum set with Zildjian cymbals. A college student without a shirt answered the door, smoking a cigarette.

"My landlord won't let me play them in the apartment," he said, gesturing to the set. Not exactly the best line for a sales pitch, I thought. He mumbled something about needing money to help pay for college.

The apartment was grimy, and the drum set was a little dirty, but I saw the potential in it. I tested the drums and the cymbals, although

I didn't know how to play a drum kit at all. He said he wanted to play it one last time before we loaded it up in the station wagon.

He put a record on and said, "Listen to this."

He played along to "Won't Get Fooled Again" by The Who as loud as he could. "I hate my landlord and neighbors," he laughed.

My father stared hard at the hazy and chaotic scene, perhaps pondering how this would all work at our house or what this would do to me. Or perhaps contemplating the existence of original sin.

We put the drum set in the far corner of the basement, near the freezer and the washer and dryer. My father hung up blankets in close proximity in an attempt to muffle the sound. I cleaned the drums, using something called "Zud" on the cymbals to make them shine.

I plugged in the old 45 player and began to play along to Neil Diamond's "Cracklin' Rosie," a number one hit in 1970. I played away thinking the song was about some exotic woman; years later, I learned that it was about a cheap wine that men drank for solace when they had no girlfriend.

I eventually played along with every record I owned. I got a book from the music store that taught some basic rhythms, and bought a used Buddy Rich record at the Treasure Mart to learn from. I eventually got a college student to give me lessons on the snare drum, and I practiced regularly. Drum rolls. Paradiddles. Flamadiddles. I even drummed without drums or sticks, on tables or on my leg with my hands. Then eventually, my lessons moved beyond the snare to the whole drum set.

I played all the different drums in the band at Slauson Junior High under the watchful eye of Mr. Long, made some progress, and in the spring of eighth grade, I even played the drum set with the band at Picnic Pops, a musical extravaganza on the grounds of Pioneer High School. It was clear that day that playing drums in the basement with a record and playing drums along with a band were two entirely separate endeavors.

And I was better as a solo basement drummer.

I stuck with it, though, and made the Concert Band in ninth grade at Pioneer and then made the Symphony Band in tenth grade. I had practiced really hard for the tryout, and fortunately, it was the one piece I could play very well.

While I got a place in the Symphony Band, I didn't really feel I belonged there. The musicians at Pioneer High School were very serious and excellent. My siblings were in this category. I was not. All of the percussionists were much better than I was. I stayed for one semester before quitting—or being asked to leave depending on what version of my meeting with Mr. Bordo, the excellent and revered band director, you choose to believe.

The dispute was over my refusal to play in the Marching Band— not because it wouldn't have been fun, as marching band provided enjoyment for many of my classmates. But I didn't want to play on Friday nights because cross-country races were on Saturday morning, and I wanted to rest up. I also didn't really have time to attend Marching Band Camp in the summer or, in fact, attend any of the marching band rehearsals after school. My unwillingness to cooperate on this matter was a sore point for Mr. Bordo, evidently—made worse by my smiling and waving to friends in the band at the one football game I attended (there was no cross-country meet that next day).

He agreed to let me stay in the band until the semester break.

I'm not sure why I didn't tell my parents about the conflict. Perhaps because I had involved them in a dispute in eighth-grade band with Mr. Long that didn't end well. Most likely, it was just that I couldn't admit to my family that I was no longer in band. I didn't want them to think I couldn't stick to something musically.

When my mom finally asked about upcoming band concerts, I knew the jig was up.

"Remember I told you about the scheduling conflict?" I told my mother, hoping she'd believe me despite her keen memory. I explained that I needed to take Driver's Ed that semester and would take it the same hour as Symphony Band. This explanation was technically accurate and seemed to work, although some course shuffling could have taken care of any real course conflict.

The fact that I had traded in my musical future for Driver's Ed didn't seem quite right to my mom, but she didn't try to verify the information, as we were well into the semester. My brother suggested that I should join the choir, as they needed some more boys to join for an upcoming musical the next year.

And rather than playing the drums in the Symphony Band, I was now in a class that had a very strange driving simulation machine. This machine made me and a classmate laugh so hard the first time we used it that it prompted the Driver's Ed teacher, Mr. Karr, to say that we needed to take this class a little more seriously.

Yet, I did not give up on my drums—it was just something that I did for myself the final years of high school. I played along with the music of the 1960s and 1970s in the basement, with the door closed. And it made me happy.

When high school was over, I needed to sell my drum set to make some money for college, so I took out a classified ad in the *Ann Arbor News*. I sold it to a kid in junior high whose parents were clearly concerned about the upcoming racket that this purchase would produce. Like the college kid before me, I played it one more time before it was sold, then packed up the drums.

I sold the kit for $250, making $50.

CHAPTER 15
Summer 1971

Pioneer Basketball School

DESPITE OUR NATION AND CITY'S social turmoil, it was the fundamentals of basketball that drew the attention of many kids in the summer of 1971. The Pioneer Basketball School was under the strict direction of Pioneer Varsity Coach Rouse, with his very short hair, high-top Converse All Stars, neatly pressed shorts, and a whistle around his neck. He was usually assisted by some varsity players; that year, they included local hero Bob Elliott—the Pioneer High center and future NBA player. The gym was filled with tube-socked, sweaty boys who wore the same shirt every day. The gym was hot and humid. By Friday, even Couch Rouse was compelled to remind us that our shirts should be washed over the weekend.

In the gym, we were drilled in the fundamentals of basketball, an obsession of mine. Kids who had finished third to ninth grades, with a wide variety of interests and abilities, worked together on every manner of drills—dribbling, the three-man weave, and my personal favorite: the pick-and-roll. We then scrimmaged until exhausted. I'm sure many parents gladly paid the fee for the eight-week program for exactly that level of exhaustion.

One of the best things about the program was meeting new kids from around the city. Pickup basketball on outdoor courts was every-where, and so, knowing kids from other schools was always useful for having games to join. Coach Rouse facilitated this social integration by lining everyone up by height and then having the smallest players paired with the tallest for two-on-two, or a small, medium, and tall player similarly assigned for three-on-three, etc.

During two-on-two, since I was one of the tallest kids, I was often assigned to a shorter player from Burns Park Elementary who had very long hair, a headband, and no basketball skills whatsoever. However, he was interesting to talk with and had a particular cynical view of life and the social networks visible at the basketball school. He made me laugh with his observations.

"How, exactly, is the 'pick-and-roll' going to help me in life?" he queried.

I was quite taken aback by this, as I viewed the pick-and-roll as an essential function and concept. When it worked, it was fabulous. However, it took a lot of practice to perfect.

Toward the end of the program, after we had received a signed certificate and group photo, my companion asked whether I would like to hang out at Burns Park later that month. I had spent little time at Burns Park, so I took him up on his offer and rode my bike over to his house one afternoon.

My introduction to the world of Burns Park that summer, a couple of weeks before seventh grade at Slauson Junior High would start, can best be captured like this: sitting in a room near a very large aquarium, reading *Mad* magazines (and discussing scenarios presented in the "Spy vs. Spy" section) while listening to selections from the original *Woodstock* album that my friend thought I really should hear. "Listen to these," he said, skipping from Carlos Santana's "Soul Sacrifice" to Jimi Hendrix's "Star Spangled Banner." When I glanced at the aquarium, the fish seemed to be stunned by the beat, swaying near each other in sync to Sly & The Family Stone's "Dance to the Music."

After this expansion of my musical knowledge, we went to the Food and Drug Mart and hung out in Burns Park. I had brought along a basketball from his garage. On the top of the hill at Burns Park, my companion confessed that he would not be returning to Pioneer Basketball School next summer. In fact, he was done with sports altogether; his parents had enrolled him in the school that summer without

Pioneer Basketball School, 1971. Top left: Coach Rouse and Bob Elliott.

consulting him. He was also quite confident that junior high would be a miserable experience.

Always a trenchant social observer, he advised me that a person that was passing by was a primary distributor of "grass" at Burns Park. I was astounded by this, given my parochial school background. After some bites of my Slim Jim, sips of Yoo-hoo chocolate soda, and a few SweeTarts, I asked him where exactly the person he had pointed out would actually get the illicit drugs.

My friend said that the dope dealer he had pointed out stole it from his older sister, who in turn stole them from their parents, who taught at the University. *A lot of interfamilial, and other, crime in the Burns Park area*, I noted to myself. The summer heat and humidity, along with the baffling combination of Yoo-hoo soda, Slim Jim, and SweeTarts, made me unable to focus on what he was actually telling me. He may have said that many U-M faculty possessed marijuana, but for some reason, I heard him say or imply that many of the faculty members were actually sellers of marijuana. I found it somewhat surprising that U-M faculty members needed to supplement their faculty income in this manner.

We went to shoot baskets, and he regaled me with funny stories about attending Burns Park Elementary School. He delighted in the absurdities of situations (which are many at age twelve). He repeated back things I told him and fired questions back at me:

"You mean to tell me that last year, at a peace protest in Berkeley, that a person put down a 'Give Peace a Chance' sign and joined his friends to rob you?"

"You thought a stamp store would be open during a riot?"

"The gang also took only one of your shoes?"

"What were you thinking?"

We talked and shot baskets for hours.

It wasn't until the day before Thanksgiving, at Discount Records, that I saw my basketball friend again. "Man, how is that pick-and-roll thing going?" he laughed. "Also, do you have a lot of money to buy stamps today?"

I laughed. He was there, he said, to get a John Coltrane album called *Transition*. "You really have to listen to this," he said. I knew nothing about jazz, and I told him I was finally going to get Sly & the Family Stone's *Greatest Hits*.

"Too optimistic," he opined. He told me Tappan Junior High was a "hassle," but he eventually admitted it was not too bad.

I had plenty to be grateful for that Thanksgiving, including the people I had been thrown together with that year on the basis of height. I was grateful for hours in a gym learning the fundamentals of basketball under a no-nonsense yet patient coach. As to the pick-and-roll, my friend was wrong about it. Very important beyond basketball: You run interference, you pivot, and you roll forward, opening yourself up to a possible pass in return. All useful concepts as I navigated junior high.

And beyond.

CHAPTER 16
Summer 1971

Cleaning the Chapel, and Street Life

WHEN WE RETURNED FROM CALIFORNIA in 1970, my brother became the janitor at my father's student chapel on campus. It was a solid church with heavy oak pews in the sanctuary and redwood gracing the tall rafters and beautiful stained-glass windows. In 1971, when the chapel began to house young people who were living on the streets of Ann Arbor, I started helping my brother clean on Saturdays. This job first entailed rousing all the people living in the basement and ushering them outside so that we could clean.

It also involved laying down the law for Saturday and Sunday behavior so that the chapel would remain clean for Sunday services. No smoking, no drinking, no drugs. Women in one area and men in the other. My brother was thirteen and I was eleven when we were put in charge of this cleaning and enforcement effort—likely a violation of child labor laws. I inherited my brother's job in 1975, when he left for college, but by then, the basement ministry had ended.

We were tasked with cleaning and providing order to the chaos. My brother was a stern enforcer. He roused everyone on Saturday mornings, and they had to leave for several hours as we set to work. He did not want to hear about late-night binges, relationships gone wrong, or other reasons people could not open their eyes early in the morning. "You should have thought about these consequences in advance," he would admonish them. I was his backup and would chime in as needed. We had a good routine, which included using powerful cleaning solutions and a large and somewhat-dangerous floor buffer that would shine the brown tile floors.

I liked the routine of cleaning, and I liked that we were down on campus amid the students and the street people and the flow of life there. Sometimes, as a reward, we would go to The Brown Jug Restaurant and get a sandwich or pizza for lunch. Or to Drake's Sandwich Shop and get a grilled pecan roll, limeade, and some double-salted Dutch black licorice for later. The black licorice discolored our mouths and tongues as we scrubbed away any dirt at the church.

Though we needed the folks out of the chapel while we cleaned, I still got to know the people who stayed there. There were different categories of people. There were young people from Michigan who may have dropped out of college—or they may have been kicked out of their homes by their parents. There were also young people who were traveling through Ann Arbor on a circuit that also included Cambridge, New York City, Boulder, and Berkeley and San Francisco.

They may have been messed up on drugs. And they were disillusioned with the state of society. There also were some recent Vietnam veterans who were in a lot of pain. My father eventually hired a graduate student—the one whose head was split open by the police during the 1968 Democratic convention—to live in the basement and provide additional supervision during the week. He had credibility on the street.

But on Saturday mornings, my brother was in charge. And many of these folks who found themselves in the basement of the chapel on Saturday morning were queried by me about their present circumstances. Between the ages of eleven and fifteen, I did not hesitate to provide advice if asked, nor did my brother. And we made it clear that between Saturday morning and Sunday evening, the chapel was going to be cleaned and remain clean. No matter how much of the city's dirt they tracked in. No matter their particular situation.

Some situations from the basement would make it back to our home. A pregnant woman who had lived in the basement for a time was at our house one day with her baby. My mom was upstairs helping this woman give the baby a bath. After the woman left, I had many

CAMPUS CHAPEL

washtenaw at
forest
services at
10:00 a.m. and **7:00 p.m.**

The Campus Chapel, 1964.

questions for my mom, who appeared to have helped show the woman several tips on childcare.

I wanted to know why the woman had even had the child and why she didn't know a lot of basic things.

My mom reminded me, "Sometimes, a lot of these questions get in the way of doing the things that need to be done." And that day, that woman needed some help, and the baby needed a bath. She concluded,

"That is all you need to know right now."

But some of the time, I was able to hear their stories directly from the people in the basement and listen to their takes on the world. And I liked to talk to them about music. Many had guitars and liked to sing on the chapel lawn. Despite being homeless, they had some records, and they would play them on a record player in the chapel basement. I was convinced that no matter their turmoil, one of them could be the next Janis Joplin or Jimi Hendrix.

After cleaning the chapel, with shriveled fingertips from the rubber gloves we wore to clean the bathrooms, it was time to go to Discount Records and go through the bins of records and talk to other people going through the bins. And time to find out about more singers that were chronicling the times we were living in. I learned about Janis Joplin from a cashier at Discount Records who had gone to her concert at Crisler Arena in 1969.

"Listen to this song," she said, when "Piece of My Heart" was playing. "Joplin's messed up and in pain, but that is some pure passion."

I wanted to meet someone who wore purple glasses and sang like that. When I heard that Joplin had died of a drug overdose in the fall of 1970, I felt compelled to say a prayer for her while in the sanctuary.

My father dropped us off on Saturdays and sometimes stayed around. But while we often invoked his name in tense situations, he wasn't often around to back us up. But I was once witness to his skill in defusing tension. One Saturday afternoon, a person was causing a lot of trouble in the basement and was threatening to burn the church down. Given that the chapel was mainly large limestone blocks, this seemed unlikely to me. Yet he was wild-eyed and looked dangerous, just the type of person in the Bible who might have been possessed by a demon.

My father came downstairs to see what the commotion was all about. The wild-eyed man had picked up a ping-pong paddle. What constituted as campus ministry work for my father evidently included playing ping-pong with students, so he had bought and set up a ping-pong table in the chapel basement. The would-be arsonist seemed angry at everyone in the world and was going to take it out on the Campus Chapel. But my father suggested that they play some ping-pong before this act of arson. My brother and I just looked at each other, recognizing the absurdity of this. I was thinking of getting a gardening tool from the janitorial closet to use as a weapon if needed.

The man said, somewhat incoherently, that if my father won, he would burn down the church. And if my father lost, he would burn down the church. There didn't seem to be much incentive for my father in this situation. Despite this scenario and the arsonist's wild demeanor, the arsonist actually could play some ping-pong. But he was no match for my father, who was quite good.

I was fascinated by the match. It was good versus evil in my view. It was a battle for the man's soul. As I watched the white ball go back and forth, it was like a little round soul that was being struggled over. Back and forth. I wanted my father to crush him. But I began to realize that my father was keeping the score close and was neither going to let him win nor lose. The tie scenario went on and on and on, and the potential arsonist finally threw his paddle down and said he was sick of the game.

But the back and forth had simply worn the anger out of him. Or perhaps the drugs were wearing off. He even thanked my father for playing with him, picked up his jacket and his backpack, and left. And he did not come back to burn the chapel down. In fact, we never saw him again. A nameless person who was just travelling through town.

So, on Saturday mornings in the 1970s, I was able to help my brother put things back in order at the chapel in the middle of the University campus despite the chaos. This cleaning ritual brought comfort. I liked to polish the tile floor and make sure the bathrooms smelled like bleach. And when I was alone upstairs in the sanctuary, I liked to make sure the hymnals and Bibles were in their proper order in the pew. Blue hymnal, red Bible, blue hymnal. And in the solitude, with the light through the stained-glass windows showing some of the dust in the air, I could hum the hymns of the ages which I had been taught.

And I could whistle and sing the passionate songs of the day that lifted my soul.

And they became eternal tones to me.

CHAPTER 17
Fall 1971

Small House and an Opportunity

IN THE SUMMER OF 1971, my parents received a letter from the Ann Arbor Public School District that placed me, and ninety-nine other kids, in an "educational pilot program" for the seventh grade. This program was to be known as Small House. It involved four teachers teaching the same students, rotating by subjects

The Ann Arbor Public Schools had been dealing with racial strife in the 1970–71 school year. There were fights among students at Pioneer High School, and the library had been damaged during unrest in October 1970. Human relations counselors were assigned to the schools at the time and roamed the hallways, working to create a sense of community and defuse racial and other tensions. AAPS also issued a report in the early 1971 called "Humaneness in Education," and the Small House teachers at Slauson Junior High worked on a program to renew students' interest in learning and to make school more "meaningful, positive and fun."

Well, perhaps.

What I was concerned about was the chaos of around nine hundred kids milling around in front of Slauson Junior High School on the first day. I was not in parochial school anymore. I was humming a combination of the James Taylor song "You've Got a Friend" and "Just My Imagination" by The Temptations as I walked toward the school entrance.

"Are those pants a protest against the war?" were the first words spoken to me that first day of school. I was wearing a new pair of red, white, and blue striped pants with some stars on them.

I replied to the sincere classmate, wearing a peace-sign belt buckle, that I was wearing them because my mom had gotten them for me at Bargain Days that summer and because "it seemed good to wear pants today." Not sure, in hindsight, that this came out right.

But those were my first words of junior high.

I met teachers who were passionate. Mrs. Green taught math. She had a calm voice that had a certain lilt, and I actually enjoyed listening to how math sounded when she spoke. She was very enthusiastic, which I greatly appreciated. She also introduced me to various math games. But my time with her was short.

One day, she wanted to talk to me alone after class. She was wearing a stylish light green dress and a matching green headband (and this alone, given her name, caused me to lose focus for a minute). After I refocused and because she was so kind, I was prepared to admit almost anything she was going to question me about or accuse me of.

"I'm doing this for your own good," Mrs. Green calmly said. She was moving me from the class. She said she had realized that I had done much of the current curriculum in the prior year, and then she got me to confess that my older brother also enjoyed teaching me math on the side. She then escorted me down the hall to put Miss Marin in charge of my math education for the next two years.

"I want you to acquit yourself well in this class," Mrs. Green said. I would do anything she said, apparently including acquitting myself, although I didn't know what that meant.

Mrs. Bridges taught Life Science. She inspired many kids to become interested in science. I was particularly impressed with her white lab coat. She liked to gesture with a dissection knife in her hand. I remember some excellent warm fall days working on frog dissection projects (and particularly, working so close to formaldehyde so close to lunch). She demanded students use correct terminology and wash their hands after her class.

Mrs. Butcher taught English and was a force of nature who had a passion for plays. In that one year, Small House put on at least two plays, *West Side Story* (which I was not in) and *Oliver!*

"You would do very well in this part," she said to me one day. That explains how I found myself in *Oliver!*, in a bit part (evidently perfect for me) as Mr. Sowerberry, the undertaker. I had one line: "I told Mr. Bumble we might consider taking in this boy Oliver to work in the shop." Parents and classmates watched this play in the sweltering June heat, adding another layer of sweat to the old red seats in the Slauson auditorium.

But the fourth teacher, Ms. Davis, had a particularly lasting impact, as she encouraged the study of current events. She taught something called "Unified Studies." We got extra credit for reports, which we could write about anything. I kept a notebook at the ready. This class, and the powerful lure of extra credit, provided an excuse to roam about town: "I'm heading downtown for current events class," I would say. My kind mother would even offer to pack a lunch for me.

Visiting campus protests, writing about them, and describing them to the class were normal events. Two specific protests drew my attention in the spring of 1972: the first annual Hash Bash in April and the "Bomb Crater" protest of the Vietnam War on the Diag in May. During the latter, four holes were dug—one on the Diag—to demonstrate the destruction in Vietnam. These highlights of Ann Arbor history and national events prompted me to wander around the city writing down bits of information to bring to class. And I knew Ms. Davis would appreciate as much detail as possible. So I provided it.

I even found the phrases "current events class project" and "extra credit" useful when dealing with various Ann Arbor police officers during this year, and future years, when questioned why, exactly, I happened to be at certain events, locations, or incidents in the city.

While there was always something new every day that year at Slauson, one thing was constant: I took exactly the same lunch every day. After the vicissitudes of Lutheran school hot lunch, I wanted complete consistency: two large peanut butter and jelly sandwiches. One apple or orange. Carrot and celery sticks. One carton of milk. And the best thing: a large slice of one of my mom's homemade breads. I soon began bringing an extra slice after I found out how valuable it was. And this had positive consequences.

I initially gave out a small piece of my mom's homemade bread when a classmate wanted to try it. I then found I could trade a slice for a Hostess Fruit Pie or a Twinkie or a Ding Dong. Those products could be further traded. Eventually, this trading operation expanded to include baseball cards and stamps. I constructed extra shelves in my locker.

The trading operation was a good way to meet new people. My mom's breads were a valuable commodity. I limited its availability to keep the value high.

Word spread.

The next year, two days after an encounter with the principal about an incident involving a Bunsen burner, I found out that even he was aware of the trading venture. He asked me point-blank if it was true that I was running a trading post out of my locker. I told him about it. I assured him that I only traded legal products. "I am also a fair trader," I said.

"This whole operation is based on your mom's baked breads?" he asked.

"Yeah, her bread is really good," I explained.

"What exactly does your mom get out of all this?" he asked.

"Well, she really likes to bake," was all I could come up with. I had not thought about this operation in those terms.

I told him I would get him a sample of her best product. He looked interested. I mentioned I was bringing in a larger shipment of banana bread later in the week for a more complicated four-way transaction.

I didn't give him the full details, but I had optioned some future deliveries of bread slices for a slightly worn Al Kaline baseball card, a three-cent commemorative stamp from 1937 of the U.S. Constitution Sesquicentennial, and a Hostess cherry pie. The deal ultimately involved other cards and products, including cinnamon-flavored toothpicks.

"Well, I suppose it wouldn't do any harm to see what this is all about," he said.

I explained to him that my mom's banana bread came in two varieties: with or without crushed walnuts.

"I am," he said, pausing thoughtfully while running a finger and thumb down his mustache, "very partial to walnuts."

I brought him a large slice later in the week.

"I can see why your venture has done well," he said after a bite.

I nodded.

CHAPTER 18
Fall 1971

Seventh-Grade Party

THE FALL OF 1971 WAS A DIFFICULT TIME in the Ann Arbor Public Schools, the city, and the nation. It appeared to me, even as a kid, that adults were simply exhausted from the concerns of the times. The Slauson Junior High building itself, built in 1937, had suffered from hard use over the prior thirty-four years. I was getting to know the kids and the lay of the building. It had perilous areas, particularly the stairways, including a circular staircase leading from the balcony in the auditorium to a bizarre room above. Yet, Slauson, as shabby and strange as it was then, seemed new and promising to me. Especially with a fall seventh-grade party on the horizon.

At this event, the seventh graders were set loose in the school at night, and they scattered while teachers and parents sought to block them from many parts of the building and maintain some sort of social order. (This general phenomenon was similar to when, inexplicably, my brother and I once let our gerbils loose in the backyard and thought we would be able to corral them simply with supervision and large wood planks.)

I had come out of parochial school and was used to a great deal of order and only one small sixth-grade class. The Small House cluster I was grouped with had one hundred kids. The seventh-grade party was a chance to meet a broader group of classmates.

There was a parental sign-up sheet announced in class, and I immediately volunteered both of my parents for this event. I may have believed that I would get some sort of extra credit for doing so. The odd thing was, I didn't find it at all strange to have invited my parents. I did find out that I was in the distinct minority on this point.

There were two concerns related to my parents and this party.

First, my mom was assigned to a craft area near the girls' bathroom. I gently broke the news to her that I doubted anyone would actually want to do crafts and that I had observed that there were girls in seventh grade who smoked and swore, both inside and outside the school. My mom took this in stride. She knew my concern about smoking, as I had written a lengthy paper in sixth grade about the Surgeon General's Report, "The Health Consequences of Smoking," which came out January 1, 1971.

Second, I found out that my father would be assigned to the recreation room. I reviewed the parental fact sheet carefully and read that they were going to have ping-pong tables set up. My father loved ping-pong, and we had a table in our basement, and he had one at his chapel. I reminded him that he wasn't there to interact with the kids and that his job was really to keep order. He didn't seem to be paying very close attention to me.

We got to the party, and I took off. Kids were indeed scurrying around. I explored the school for quite a while with various groups, and then I went to the gym to watch classmates roller skate. From a room off the gym, there was a large supply of musty roller skates for kids to use to skate on the worn gym floor. I wasn't a very good skater, but I enjoyed observing some of my classmates' significant skating ability. Until, that is, a new (and quite irritating) song referencing roller skates came on: "Brand New Key" by Melanie. The song was somewhat jarring and drove me from the gym.

From there, I met up with some other kids, and we roamed over to check out the auditorium, where an old Vincent Price horror movie was playing: *House of Usher*. This was a freaky movie.

I had heard a rumor that kids might be making out in the balcony area of the auditorium and also drinking Boone's Farm Strawberry Hill Wine. I went up to check this out. And there were many other kids investigating these rumors but no actual participants in these activities at that time.

For the first time, I found the metal winding staircase (the one that went up to a hidden room), but given the eerie mood of the movie and having seen many episodes of *The Twilight Zone*, I decided not to explore it.

Leaving the auditorium, I met up with a classmate who excitedly reported that some kids were trying to beat my father in the rec room. I, naturally, was concerned about this and went to see it for myself. There, I saw a line of kids near one of the ping-pong tables.

My father was not, it appeared to me, properly monitoring the game room. Instead, he was playing ping-pong (with his own paddle, which he had evidently smuggled from our house, undetected by me). There was a long line of kids watching. The game was winner-stays-in. My best friend in seventh grade came and told me that no one had been able to beat my dad yet. He seemed to think my dad was pretty cool for doing this. I watched my dad—his long hair and beard making him look like a campus radical of the time—keep the games close, encourage even the worst player, and teach the game but not let any kid win.

Seeing that my dad was not being beaten—at ping-pong or in any other way—I moved on to sample other activities.

I checked in on the lunchroom dance area, where The Jackson 5's "ABC" pulsated. There were mainly girls on the dance floor, and many were excellent dancers. A girl I knew came over and asked me why the boys didn't really want to dance. My response was simply, "I don't know." For seventh-grade boys, "I don't know" or outright denial were likely the two most common responses to almost any inquiry— thus providing as little information or detail as possible.

The influx of information in junior high was so great, yet providing information took significant effort.

The girl pressed me, and I said, "They don't really know how to dance, or they have never danced before."

She looked at me and said, "Now tell me, here, have you ever danced with a girl before?"

"I don't know," I responded. My unease and her close proximity caused me to yawn, and as I did, the small rubber bands attached to my upper and lower braces popped out of my mouth as if to highlight the foolishness of this answer. I tried to catch them in midair.

She laughed and then looked straight at me, and in a disarming way, she said, "I don't know you very well, but you might want to pay a little more attention to things if you don't know whether or not you have ever danced with a girl."

"I suppose so," was all I could muster in response.

After a moment of reflection, I went up the stairs, and things took a strange turn.

Another girl rushed by, an unlit cigarette in her mouth. I knew her from Small House. She thrust a brown paper bag in my hands and asked me to hold it for her. I nodded but did not really have time to consent fully—I just ended up holding the bag. After she ran off, an adult monitor turned the corner and went after her.

I went to another area to peek into the bag. I feared that the circumstance I was now in was a variation of what I had vaguely been warned about in parochial school: girls running by and handing off paper bags full of their problems. Of course I was right. The bag held a carton of Virginia Slims cigarettes. She was clearly a dealer of some sort.

I thought hard about what to do with this situation. Should I turn this over to the principal? While I contemplated further, I went to see how my mom was holding up in the craft area. I assumed she was probably feeling left out because no one would really want to do crafts at a party. To my amazement, my mom had a group of girls around her learning to crochet.

And some of these girls were the exact girls that I had warned my mom about—the ones who smoked and swore—yet, they all listened quite carefully to her as she spoke to them in her calm way. Moreover, *there* was the girl that had dumped the bag on me. She had obviously just sat down to watch while hiding out from the monitor. In a place least likely to be found.

As I left the craft area, I put the bag next to the girl while maintaining some strong eye contact with my mom, who watched me transfer the package. I went back later and saw my mom talking to the girl alone, so I left them to it as I went to get my dad. When we met my mom outside the party, I noticed that my mom now had the paper bag. She casually tossed it in the trash can in the parking lot outside before we got to the car.

My mom said that she couldn't quite imagine how I came into possession of that particular bag. I said it wasn't really clear to me either; I was just standing around, and things had happened rather quickly. My father asked about what we were discussing. My mom paused.

Rather than answer, I instead asked him whether it had really been necessary for him to bring his own ping-pong paddle to the party. And in a fancy leather carrying case.

In the fall of 1971 in Ann Arbor, there were about three hundred kids passing through Slauson seventh grade at the same place and time—some of whom I got to know well and some of whom I watched from afar. And someone who reminded me to pay closer attention to things in life.

I thought about what I had observed at the party while we rode home in our old station wagon—down South Seventh, past the high school and Pioneer Woods, to the darkness of Scio Church Road, to our home on Covington. Watching this part of the city out the window, the fall air flowing in, I hummed Motown tunes to myself, thinking, all in all, my first seventh-grade party had gone pretty well.

Even with my parents there.

CHAPTER 19
December 1971

The Free John Sinclair Concert

I RECEIVED A LETTER FROM Slauson Junior High, dated June 20, 1972, requesting that my parents ensure payment of two dollars for rebinding a math book that was allegedly damaged in my custody during the just-completed seventh-grade year.

A bullying incident caused my math book to sustain initial damage. It took place soon after I joined the new math class (a mixed eighth-ninth-grade class). Because I was the youngest kid in the math class and didn't know anyone, I sat in the back of the class and kept to myself. I sat near a girl whom I had seen get dropped off at school by someone on a motorcycle. She wore an army jacket and leather boots. I had seen her out smoking. I somehow imagined, unfairly perhaps, that she might be carrying a knife in her boot—something I had seen on TV.

She came up to me in the Slauson library and asked if she could copy my homework. She indicated that she would "make it worth my while." I looked at her carefully. What exactly was this all about? The idea of cheating generally bothered me. But I wasn't perfect. I had, in the past, been willing to trade basic answers to worksheet questions on the book *Animal Farm* for snacks.

But math was quite different, and I viewed it as the purest form of knowledge. Because of her rough demeanor, I was concerned that she was going to try to give me cigarettes or alcohol or drugs.

SLAUSON JUNIOR
HIGH SCHOOL
•
1019 W. WASHINGTON ST.
ANN ARBOR, MICH. 48103
TELEPHONE 9-0826
•
COLLIER E. OWENS
PRINCIPAL

ANN ARBOR PUBLIC SCHOOLS

ANN ARBOR -:- MICHIGAN

June 20 1972

Steve Postema - 7

Dear Parents:

Your son or daughter has either lost or damaged one or more textbooks. Listed below are the name(s) of t h e textbook(s), whether they were lost or damaged, and the charge for each one. Your cooperation in seeing that the books are paid for by the end of the school year, June 16th, would be a p p r e c ia te d.

rebinding math book $2.00

If you have any questions, please feel free to call.

Sincerely,

Dianne Hendershott
Assistant Principal - AM

Tom Johns
Assistant Principal - PM

Slauson Damaged Book Letter, June 1972. Signed by not one but two Slauson Assistant Principals.

Echoing something I had heard from Mr. Siano, the kind counselor for Small House, I replied that, with cheating, she would only be cheating herself. Her look of disdain clued me that she was quite content to cheat herself and that she didn't really appreciate my attitude. I tried another tack. I liked to help people in math, so I offered to simply work with her on her math homework. In response, I believe she uttered the word "freak," then shoved my math book on the floor and left. This caused the initial tear in the spine binding. This girl scowled at me occasionally but otherwise left me alone for the year.

Although I had duct-taped the book's spine, the most serious damage was sustained while trying to sneak into the "Free John Sinclair" concert at Crisler Arena on December 10, 1971. I was unaware of the social significance of this concert, and it might surprise many people that I would have tried to attend a marijuana related rally at all, but all I knew was that John Lennon was going to sing and that it might be worthwhile to see him. (It turns out, he was so late; he didn't sing until two or three in the morning.) But even more important, I really wanted to see Stevie Wonder and Bob Seger, who were also playing.

The concert focused on the injustice of Sinclair's long prison sentence for minor marijuana possession. Three days after the concert, the Michigan Supreme Court issued an order that directed Sinclair be released on bond. Several months later, the same court found the state of Michigan's marijuana law to be unconstitutional.

However, I never got into the famous concert. I didn't have a ticket, but there was a rumor that a classmate's uncle was working as security and was going to let that classmate slip in a certain door. I stopped at a friend's house for dinner after school (which is why I had my math book in my backpack), and then I went to see if I could get in that certain door. This rumor about a way into the concert must have been widely spread around, as there were many kids milling around. The door was never opened (or perhaps we were at the wrong door).

Some security men came out to disperse the now-large crowd that had gathered, and in the jostling, the math book came out of my backpack (which wasn't fully zipped). I frantically crawled around trying to grab the book as it was kicked and trampled. As I picked it up, another classmate paused and asked why, exactly, I was bringing an algebra book to a rock concert.

He left before I could clear this up.

I made the trek home from Crisler Arena with my friend. We made a detour first and easily got into Michigan's football stadium.

We went down the steps onto the field in the dark. We found a tennis ball and passed it back and forth like a football. Sprinting around in the cold on the U-M field, making game-winning plays in the dark to the delight of ourselves and the shadows, eased the disappointment of not getting into the concert at Crisler.

My friend and I parted at the stadium, and I began to run home, cutting through the high school property over to Scio Church Road, because my ears were cold. When I got home that night, my mom asked where my hat was and what I had been doing since school let out. I told her I left my hat at school and responded that I was just hanging out with friends. This short phrase, over time, would become a stock answer to a wide range of activities, incidents, and behaviors.

My friend was disappointed that we had not gotten in and offered me another opportunity to see a good concert. The Grateful Dead was going to be playing at Hill Auditorium for two nights the coming week. His uncle would be working security and would be able to sneak us in, "For sure this time," he promised.

I was not particularly interested in the Grateful Dead, although I knew they were popular. I just didn't feel their music had a good enough beat like Creedence Clearwater Revival. Furthermore, I didn't trust his uncle to come through. And finally, it would be on a school night, and I had math homework. My friend went without me, came late to school the next day—as he had overslept—and said that I had missed a great concert.

Later in June, upon receipt of the damaged book letter and a discussion with my mom about proper regard for school property, my mom took me to Slauson to pay the fee. I was required to pay this out of my savings.

She also wanted me to personally apologize to the school for causing the damage, as it reflected poorly on our family. After the debt was satisfied, we drove home, but we stopped at A&W Root Beer on Stadium first.

We sat in the car talking over the past year, drinking root beer floats. The radio was playing Don McLean's "American Pie."

"What's this song all about?" she asked. I told her I wasn't sure, but I sure liked the tune.

My mom agreed that this had been quite a year. "Now tell me again what happened to that book at Crisler Arena?"

"Really. It all happened very fast."

And that was true of seventh grade too.

CHAPTER 20
April 1972

First Hash Bash

"I HATE MY PARENTS, THAT'S why I left home," the young woman told me while I was cleaning the women's restroom of the chapel in March of 1972.

I was almost thirteen, and I was wiping down the sink and toilet with strong-smelling bleach.

"Less piss on the floor in the women's room I bet," she commented. She was sitting on a small couch that was just outside the open door of the bathroom I was cleaning. She was wearing wide bell-bottoms and a U-M sweatshirt. She was skinny, she talked fast, and her eyes darted back and forth when she spoke.

"Why do you hate your parents?" I asked.

"Because they kicked me out of the house for smoking weed."

She had found her way into the chapel basement earlier that year. She said she was nineteen and from outside Grand Rapids. I talked to her sometimes on Saturdays when I cleaned with my brother. She had a guitar and often sang songs from Carole King's recent album *Tapestry*.

"That Carole King, she is a strong woman," she explained. "She changes herself over time. She just keeps going."

I told her Carole King had just won many Grammy Awards for "You've Got a Friend" and the whole album.

"Good for her. Now tell me again why your dad lets people stay down here?"

"He thinks young people sometimes need a place to stay when they have troubles," I explained.

"He is right about that. I am troubled," she laughed. "Your dad. He causes you trouble too, right? Makes your brother and you clean up after us messy and troubled people?"

"No, no, we like to work. We make money. He doesn't force us."

"But you guys are around here alone on Saturday, and some of the people around campus aren't good people or even safe to be around. Aren't you worried?"

"Not really," I said, "I can take care of myself." It did not sound convincing, so I added, "Plus, I know a police officer."

That was the first time I had thought of the people in the chapel basement as anything but harmless and in need of direction.

She began talking about some event that would take place soon on campus because the Michigan Supreme Court had ruled that the state felony law about marijuana was illegal. I told her I knew about this because I had unsuccessfully tried to attend the Free John Sinclair concert in December.

She explained that there was a new law that made marijuana possession a lesser crime, a misdemeanor. But the new law didn't take effect until April 3, 1972, creating a short time period with no state law against marijuana. To celebrate, students were going to have a first "Hash Festival" on the Diag on April 1, 1972. I worked again that Saturday—April Fool's Day. I saw the young woman, and as I was cleaning the bathrooms, she came over to tell me something:

"I'm going to make a trade."

She told me her former boyfriend had brought her a package earlier this week. He had asked her to bring it to the festival on Saturday and give it to a man at the center of the Diag, on the steps of the graduate library, at 1:00 p.m. Then she would get a package from him in return.

"Would you come over and watch me do this? I don't trust this guy."

As it got closer to 1:00 p.m., I grabbed a pen and a notebook I kept for Unified Studies and ran over to the Diag. There were a couple

Hash Bash, April 1974. Bentley Historical Library, University of Michigan.

hundred people milling around. Some people had signs. The students were eyeing the police. As I was walking, a familiar voice asked me what I was doing. Our neighbor Officer Fleming caught up with me and told me I shouldn't be here.

"What have I told you about what goes on over here on campus?"

I told him I was looking around because I would be writing about the festival for extra credit. My teacher loved current events.

"Extra credit, well that's okay then," he said as his eyes scanned the crowd. He told me to leave soon. I told him I was working over at the chapel.

I moved near the library, made some notes in my notebook, and eventually watched as the young woman gave a man in a black leather jacket a satchel and received a paper bag in return. I followed her back to the chapel. She told me that the man on the Diag had said that her former boyfriend had been arrested in Grand Rapids. He wouldn't be showing up to pick up the envelope right away.

"What was in the package you gave him?"

"Probably weed. I never looked in it."

"Can't have drugs at the chapel," I admonished weakly.

"It's gone," she laughed, adding, "there was no state law against it last week."

She went into the women's restroom with the package. When she came out, she whispered to me, "Shit. Nine hundred dollars. Nine one-hundred-dollar bills."

"That's a lot," I said.

She worried aloud, "What should I do with it?"

"You know, this really is your money," I suggested. She had told me earlier that her former boyfriend had made her take all her college money out of the bank before they came to Ann Arbor. He had most of it, and she was almost out of the money that she had left.

She bit her lip and nodded. "He's a creep. I need to get out of Michigan." She explained that her sister had encouraged her to come out to California if she needed to.

"Why not? You should."

"Well, my older sister is strict and will likely make me go to church and get a job."

"That's not all bad." The words flew out of my mouth like I was an old person.

"Promise me you'll never take drugs," she said with weariness. "I'm a frickin' mess."

I promised, and it wasn't hard given what I had observed in the chapel basement and on campus.

"You're going to go to your sister, right?"

"I will," she promised. "I swear to God here in this church basement."

I didn't say anything. She looked at me. She seemed irritated when I didn't answer.

"Damn. Do I have to swear this upstairs in the sanctuary?"

I said I believed her.

She got out the yellow pages and looked up travel agencies. Then I walked with her over to Nickels Arcade, home to Boersma Travel. I assured her that, being Dutch, this agency was likely very reliable.

"Is that so?" she said.

I waited outside while she went to buy a ticket. When she returned, she looked somewhat relieved. She said she felt strange with all this money in her purse.

I gave her one more unsolicited piece of advice: "I once told strangers I had a lot of money. For stamps. In Berkeley, California. And they stole all my money. And one shoe."

"That's strange," she said, "why only one shoe?"

"Berkeley is a strange place," I warned obliquely. *Oakland was a little safer, perhaps. And she would be with her sister*, I thought to myself.

"Yeah, the plane leaves tonight," she said. She showed me the ticket. One way. She explained that she had her sister's phone and address and that she would take a taxi to the airport. She said she had never been on a plane.

We walked back to the chapel. She got her stuff, which all fit in a large beaded purse and a backpack, except her guitar that she carried separately. She picked up her sleeping bag and went outside.

"I tossed it," she said when she came back. "Honestly, I think it has bedbugs."

I told her we had a spray for that here at the chapel. One for lice too.

She asked me to watch her meager possessions while she went to take a shower in a makeshift steel shower in the large janitorial supply closet.

After a long shower, she came back smelling of pungent shampoo. Someone had left this new type of green shampoo, Herbal Essence, in the shower. The smell was a little too much for me, but I didn't say anything.

"I feel like a new person," she said. "What is that church word for this?"

"'Purified,' maybe. Or 'sanctified.'"

"Yeah, yeah. That's it. I'm ready to leave now. Sanctified."

I walked with her to the Michigan Union. I told her there were always taxis there. She handed me five dollars for being helpful.

"What are you going to do with it?"

I told her I was going to get Carole King's *Tapestry* album.

"Cool," she said, "that is a really good album."

She waved to me out the window of the yellow taxi, mouthing, "Thanks."

I headed down State Street to Discount Records to talk to the clerks and get *Tapestry*. I then went back to the chapel to clean.

I hadn't gotten much work done yet that afternoon

CHAPTER 21
May 1972

The 600-Yard Run

IN SEVENTH GRADE, I LEARNED that it was my patriotic duty to run fast. In 1966, President Lyndon B. Johnson's President's Council established the Presidential Physical Fitness Award Program to measure the physical fitness of young people in the country.

I assumed that this was related somehow to the Great Society program that he announced in Ann Arbor in 1964. If you performed in the top eighty-fifth percentile of each of seven tests, you would get a certificate signed by the president, and most importantly, a blue patch. The seven tests were: (1) pull-ups (boys) or flexed-arm hang (girls), (2) sit-ups, (3) shuttle run, (4) standing broad jump, (5) 50-yard dash, (6) softball throw for distance, and (7) 600-yard run.

This program had its origin with President Eisenhower, and then, President Kennedy ramped up national concern about physical fitness by writing an article entitled "The Soft American," published in *Sports Illustrated*. "… the harsh fact of the matter is that there is also an increasingly large number of young Americans who are neglecting their bodies—whose physical fitness is not what it should be—who are getting soft."

I did not want to be soft. In addition, because of the Space Race with the Russians, I was concerned that the Russians were getting into much better shape. And my concern had good cause, as the Russians eventually dominated the Olympic medal count in the 1972 Summer Olympics.

But in the fall of 1971, we were being tested at Slauson Junior High in gym class, along with everyone else in the nation. I had it in my mind that this test information would be entered into a federal database. I certainly wanted to look good for the federal government, particularly if my neighbor Congressman Marvin Esch were, at some point, to review this data in Washington, D.C.

Of all of these tests, it was the 600-yard run that caused the most dread among students. Everyone in junior high was moaning about this run. But I was looking forward to it. Having run all over town since kindergarten and having competed in running races in elementary school, the distance seemed very short to me. It was my patriotic duty to do well on this test. Moreover, I was motivated to get the badge. And I did. My mom sewed it on my favorite jacket.

I did particularly well on the 600-yard run, and the gym teacher, Mr. Singh, encouraged me to join the track team. He had been on the Indian Olympic team, and he believed that running was the key to success in life. Although he was a small man, he knew judo and was able to keep kids in line well, and he even managed to disarm a large new boy who had brought a handgun to the locker room.

I was impressed by this.

I was a willing convert to Mr. Singh's life view. He pointed out that, in the track meets that spring, I would be able to run against all the kids in the city. He said I could become the fastest seventh grader in the city if I worked at it. This certainly had great appeal to me.

I dedicated myself to training for the 600-yard run, the longest distance race for seventh graders. I measured out a 600-yard course on the sidewalk around the block at home and practiced at night after track practice. Plus, I began to run my entire weekly paper route. I did not have running shoes, so I ran in my low-top basketball shoes.

As I was browsing at Discount Records, one of the salesclerks wondered where I had been lately, and I told him I was busy training for track meets. And I complained about my lack of running shoes. I also confessed that I had bought some really cheap albums from the Treasure Mart's deeply discounted bins. I promised him I would be back for some albums later in the summer when I had some more money.

He told me that it would be good to have a song to inspire me while I trained. "This will get you going," he said, and then played "Run Run Run" by The Who, a song from 1966. I didn't really understand the lyrics, but I liked the refrain and the beat, which encouraged everyone to run. I thanked him for the information.

I was humming the refrain of the song at my first track meet at Tappan Junior High, standing on a grass field behind a white chalk line. I looked across the starting line and saw a kid who had beautiful long hair down to his shoulders, held back with a colored headband. My hair was also long but thin and hard to control. I wore an unattractive headband, which looked like it was made out of the same material as my jockstrap, to keep my hair under control when I ran. As the race started, all I could think about was how much I wished I had hair like my competitor's.

All the more incentive to beat him in this race. And I did.

We raced against each other again at the all-city meet at the end of the season. It was held on a hot afternoon at the U-M outdoor track. While waiting to race, a ninth grader on the Slauson team told me that I couldn't possibly win with the bulky shoes I had on. He asked me what size shoe I wore. I wore the same size as he did, it turned out. He said that I could wear his on one condition: "You must promise to win by a large margin."

"How large of a margin?" I asked.

"No one anywhere near you," he said.

I agreed to this because I had to get the shoes. These shoes were not just running shoes but actual white racing shoes with small spikes. They felt like slippers when I put them on. I felt like Hermes, the Greek messenger to the Gods, with winged sandals. And I needed to deliver a message fast.

My coach had said to start sprinting at the 440-yard mark. "Think of something chasing you," he had said. In some earlier races, I had thought about some of the bad dogs on my paper route, and this imagery had worked to a certain extent. But for this race, I brought out an even more primal fear. At the 440-yard mark, I thought about what still terrified me, and I heard my brother's voice from when we

had lived in California: "The Zodiac serial killer is coming for you."
And then I heard The Who telling me to run, run, run.

I won by a very large margin.

I gave the shoes back to my older teammate.

"Good job," he said, "but man, you looked like you were freaking out coming toward the finish line."

"Believe me," I said, "I was."

CHAPTER 22
May 1972

Small House Science Camp

THE PEACEFUL STATE OF NATURE, contemplated by the philosopher Jean-Jacques Rousseau, existed at Camp Innisfree, an educational camp within the National Lakeshore State Forest, beautifully situated on a bluff above Lake Michigan, near Sleeping Bear Dunes. But it was seriously tested when, near the end of the 1971 school year, seventh graders from Slauson Small House got off the school bus.

Six hours earlier, I was busy contemplating two contrasting musical views of the world while I waited to load onto the bus at Zion Lutheran Church; this location, two blocks from school, was clearly being used to prevent the other kids at Slauson from being jealous that we were the only group to go on this desirable five-day educational excursion.

Near the bus, three girls were singing the first thought-provoking song with their arms linked together. It was about harmony in the world, and it was called "I'd Like to Teach the World to Sing" by The Hillside Singers, which had evolved from a song in a famous Coca-Cola commercial. The world harmonizing together was a good message at the time. We had sung the song in choir that year.

The second song was, in jarring contrast, Alice Cooper's "School's Out." It had just been released. And this song made me laugh because it was so absurd and dysfunctional and appealing to a certain segment of junior high students: it talked about lack of class, principles, and innocence. The refrain rang out with anarchy and celebrated that school would be out forever.

Seventh grade oscillated wildly between harmony and chaos. I met many friends and had three special confidants, but I made some enemies, including one who carried a knife. I loved the structures of math, but I couldn't draw straight lines with little arrows on light green engineering paper if my life depended on it and was moved out of the mechanical drawing class after only a quarter.

I was put in choir, and that was a better fit.

I was taking stock of my year as I watched classmates get dropped off. There was drama going on regarding who some of the girls would sit with on the bus. This was having a ripple effect. I had my good friend to sit with. He had red hair, wore a Pope Paul medallion on a necklace, and he had a quick wit and an easy smile. He also had a great ability to mimic teachers and school administrators, so it was always entertaining to be around him.

When we arrived at camp, we were told by the staff that campers were encouraged to do what they wanted, that it was a self-directed camp. I wondered if these adults fully understood the ramifications of the freedom they were prescribing. After all, on the trip up, I had witnessed a chaotic scene as the school bus stopped for gas at a station with a convenience store attached. I then fully understood why most such gas stations heading up north had signs that said no school buses allowed.

I wasn't present when the interaction happened, but evidently, very soon into our stay, a parent-chaperone nicknamed Mr. Scar (a shortened version of his long Italian name) had confiscated a wrist rocket from a classmate who was engaging in the self-directed activity of shooting out light bulbs near the front of the cabins. A wrist rocket was an amped-up and powerful version of a slingshot, and it could do serious damage. In the cabin, the boy and his friends complained because the list of prohibited items in the camp paperwork included slingshots but did not mention wrist rockets specifically.

I was asked for my opinion, as were others, about this travesty of justice.

"I would classify a wrist rocket as a type of slingshot," I replied truthfully. "Anyway, the list of prohibited items also says 'any other type of dangerous weapon.'" So, I opined that the chaperone was fully entitled to confiscate the wrist rocket.

This analysis was not well received by some of my cabinmates who insisted that the whole cabin should fight the parent to show solidarity. This did not seem like a good plan to me, again, having examined the list of rules that I had brought along, as it could result in expulsion from camp. Despite being disappointed by my opinion, my cabinmates still asked if I saw any way around these rules.

Because we had been told that we could come up with our own activities, I recommended instead that we have two boys wrestle the chaperone for the return of this wrist rocket. If in the heat of wrestling other contact occurred, well, then at least there would be a plausible defense against an assault charge. Many thought this was a good idea and asked if I could arrange it because I knew Mr. Scar.

Facing the *Lord of the Flies* situation before me, I agreed, although I was opposed to this whole venture, even the very wrestling scheme that I had proposed. I liked Mr. Scar, as he had been a chaperone at the local science camp that fall. He had cooked spaghetti with my mother in the kitchen at that camp, and I got to know him.

Our counselor then walked in. He was a medical school student and brother of one of my classmates. We told him about the wrestling challenge. He had no firm opinion on it. But he showed his true value as a counselor when, later that evening, he gave a truly graphic sex education talk after hearing some of the boys incorrectly describing some sexual activity. This talk was so detailed and informative that the cabin got little sleep that night.

But before that was a group discussion about which two boys would wrestle Mr. Scar. This discussion was surprisingly focused and rational for seventh-grade boys, but finally, two of the bigger boys who were on the wrestling team were selected.

I relayed this challenge to Mr. Scar, who seemed amused by the whole prospect. He didn't exactly say no, so I relayed that the challenge had been accepted. And the next day, on the top of Sleeping Bear Dunes with the vastness of Lake Michigan to the west, a large circle of boys watched a grown man take on two boys in the sand. Eventually, Mr. Scar had them face down in the sand with firm hands on their necks. They were squirming but largely immobilized.

And I was quite happy about this.

Mr. Scar then charitably released them, saying that this seemed to be a draw, in his view. Our counselor strolled by at that minute and asked whether there was any trouble. Mr. Scar said no, that the boys were just messing around. While likely against all existing Ann Arbor school-chaperone protocol, it was clear to me that this physical restraint was exactly what was needed at this camp with few rules.

It was a self-directed camper activity after all.

I was fully relieved about the return to moral order. And the boys of the cabin all agreed that, even though Mr. Scar was not going to give the wrist rocket back, he was a pretty cool dad to agree to this wrestling match at all. He went from being cursed to being praised.

On the ride back to Ann Arbor, I sat with my red-haired friend, and we ruminated over the activities of the trip—capture the flag, the beach, night nature walks, the sex education tutorial, and the dune-top wrestling match with Mr. Scar. Some girls were softly singing "I'd Like to Teach the World to Sing." But almost the entire bus was sleeping, knocked out from four nights in a cabin and a surplus of physical activity and fresh air.

I appreciated the harmony of the sleeping bus and having a good friend to sit with, as well as another confidant in the row ahead to share details of the trip with. But as Alice Cooper had sung, school would be out for summer soon, and I had learned that potential anarchy was always lurking nearby.

CHAPTER 23
June 1972

———

Extra Credit Report

AFTER WE GOT BACK FROM CAMP INNISFREE, I turned my attention to an extra credit project Ms. Davis had offered to the Unified Studies class earlier in the semester: write about something local that was in the news. I chose to do a report on something that I had read about in the newspaper the prior summer and that I was aware of from as far back as 1968.

The U.S. Supreme Court had decided to review a legal case from Ann Arbor that was related to the government wiretapping of telephones. I considered myself somewhat of an expert in wiretapping because it happened every week on my favorite TV spy show, *Mission: Impossible*.

For the bombing of the CIA building on Main Street in Ann Arbor in September 1968, the United States government brought criminal charges against a member of the White Panther Party. Other members of the White Panther Party, including John Sinclair, were also charged with destruction of government property. I wrote about this case for some extra credit, adding, for color, commentary about how I had attempted to sell large candy bars to the members hanging out on the front porch of the White Panther Party headquarters (which had been renamed the "Rainbow People's Party") on Hill Street that year.

Neither the White Panthers nor the Rainbow People present on the porch that day wanted any large candy bars to support the educational venture I was promoting for a school trip. One of them even called me a pawn in a corrupt enterprise, referring to the candy bar sales, and he may have been onto something.

But, in my opinion, nothing really suspicious seemed to be going on there, despite the government charges.

The defense attorneys in the wiretapping case had sought government disclosure of all electronic surveillance information. The attorney general of the United States claimed that he didn't have to disclose this information, as he would just authorize the wiretaps under the Omnibus Crime Control and Safe Streets Act of 1968. The Act allowed for wiretapping in instances where the government believed that it was crucial to prevent the overthrow of the government.

Judge Damon Keith of the federal district court in Detroit ordered the U.S. government to disclose all of the illegally obtained conversations to the defendants. The government appealed, but the U.S. Court of Appeals rejected the government's arguments.

The U.S. Supreme Court had agreed to take the case in June 1971, and it seemed to be taking its sweet time deciding this case—I wanted to give the results in my report, but I had to submit the report before the Supreme Court ruled. In the meantime, I was very cautious on the telephone. I didn't want anything I said to be misconstrued in case the government was targeting our house.

It was only after school ended for the year that the Supreme Court upheld the prior rulings in the case, holding that the wiretaps were an unconstitutional violation of the Fourth Amendment and, as such, had to be disclosed to the defense. This established the important principle that a warrant was necessary before beginning electronic surveillance, even if domestic security issues were involved.

I was reminded of the case the next summer when my father was invited to a summer gathering of primarily Black political leaders, judges, and power brokers in Detroit. My father was none of these but had been invited through church connections. My father, a pastor, was even invited to give a prayer.

Outside, I watched as a distinguished man tended to a grill. People gravitated toward him and spoke with him. He seemed to be dispensing wisdom at the grill. My father told me it was Judge Keith of the federal court. I moved closer to where he was grilling.

At one point, when he was alone, he pointed at me with his grilling tongs and asked what I thought of the party. I told him the food was pretty good, and I was there with my dad, who had said the prayer.

"Your father had a good prayer."

"Seemed maybe a little long to me."

The judge laughed. "Not compared to ones in the churches I go to," he said, "particularly given the state of the country right now."

I told him I knew about his wiretap case. He asked me how I came to know about such a case. I told him I was from Ann Arbor and had written about the case for a seventh-grade report for extra credit.

"Extra credit, that's pretty good," he said.

He asked where I had gotten my information. I told him I had gotten it from the newspapers. And because the judge (who would eventually become one of the most distinguished federal judges on the Sixth Circuit U.S. Court of Appeals) had such a powerful presence, even as he was just casually cooking on the grill, I suddenly felt obligated to confess something to him on the spot.

Since he had asked about my sources, I told him that I had actually copied much of my report word for word from those newspapers.

He paused, pointing the grilling tongs at me again, "Just put it in your own words next time, and cite your sources, then you'll be okay."

I felt relieved, if not fully absolved.

And I told him I would do just that.

CHAPTER 24
Summer 1972

Fuller Pool and Bargain Days

THE SUMMER OF 1972 CAME just as seventh grade had ended. The first day of summer, I rode my recently purchased ten-speed Sierra Brown Schwinn Varsity bike—no-handed, as often as possible—to Fuller Pool. I purchased the bike at Kiddie Korner, the Schwinn bike shop on the corner of Main and Madison, one block down from the CIA building that had been bombed in 1968. The price for the bike and a lock was ninety-three dollars. I did not buy a bike helmet because they did not yet exist.

I had gone to the Huron Valley National Bank the day before to withdraw a one-hundred-dollar bill from my savings. The teller, who knew our family, called my mom to see if the withdrawal was permitted. This bothered me; it was, after all, my own money. Hard-earned money, at that, from four jobs.

My new bike replaced a completely impractical five-speed Sting-Ray, which had a very small front wheel, large handlebars, and an elongated banana seat. The bike was called the "Pea Picker" because of its green color. Schwinn Sting-Rays were all the rage in the 1960s. They were good for popping wheelies but not great for long-distance riding. It was a kid's bike. I needed something new.

My new bike expanded my range in the city. I spent more time at Veterans Park Pool, as it was closer, but it was always worthwhile to meet new kids at Fuller, a much larger pool, making the longer ride worth it. Some kids were friendly, some were not. On this particular afternoon, a group of boys in the locker room was evidently quite amused by what I happened to be wearing.

Let me give some context to my situation: Growing up in a home of modest means, my mother would take us downtown in hot and sticky July to get special bargains on clothes at the outdoor sales that stores on State and Main Street had during the summer Art Fair. Bins of deeply discounted clothing. Racks of potential deals.

My mom was very thrifty and would carefully sift through the dross. Upon closer inspection, some of the clothes she found were slightly off—perhaps the buttons didn't quite align, perhaps the collar was crooked, and sometimes the colors were, well, interesting. A pair of blue and red canvas platform shoes was more appropriate for Elton John than me.

"They were free," my mom said.

Of course they were.

These oddities were things that other kids picked up on. This became clear in the Fuller Pool locker room that day when one of boys let loose: "Boy, where did you get those clothes? Did your mother dress you?"

Never one to shy away from discussion, I engaged. I began to earnestly explain that my mother had, in fact, gotten these clothes for me at Bargain Days the past summer.

"Hey, my mom is a good shopper," I emphasized.

I then detailed the exact stores where each item could be purchased, if they were so inclined. After providing some clear amusement to this group, and defending my mother's purchases, they left, and I took a closer examination of my serious sartorial situation in the locker room mirror.

I was wearing a wide, horizontal-striped, green and white t-shirt, which would have been normal, but the stripes themselves were not quite even. My wide bell-bottom pants were thin, multicolored, and vertically striped, but these stripes, too, were defectively printed on the fabric. Visually, the combination was disorienting—jarring, in fact.

And my socks. The prior summer, my mom had bought a deeply

discounted package of twenty-four socks, for my dad, brother, and me, that were the exact color of Circus Peanuts candy. This bag of socks was as big as a pillow and probably cost a quarter, about a penny a pair. The bag of socks was still available because not one person in the entire city had found them acceptable to purchase. The socks were quite comfortable, but looking in the mirror that day, I realized that they were, in fact, very peculiar, particularly in combination with the other clothes.

I was then alone with one remaining older boy in the locker room, likely a high school junior or senior. He saw me observing myself in the mirror. "Ignore them," he said calmly, "they're just messing with you."

He asked me what grade I was going into. After I told him, he said to wear whatever I wanted and ignore any comments. While putting lotion on his arms, he did advise me to give some thought to color combinations.

But his more important bit of advice, given while combing his hair with an Afro pick, was this: Definitely get a Levi's denim jacket because it would make anyone feel very good every day in eighth grade. This made quite an impression.

He reiterated, waving the hair pick for emphasis: "I'm telling you, man, you need to get yourself a LEVI'S. JEAN. JACKET."

He was a kind, temporary friend in the locker room—I never got his name, and never saw him again. I rode home that summer day from Fuller Pool, mostly no-handed, humming a tune that had just come out a couple of months before and had gotten a lot of play on the radio. It was Bill Withers' "Lean on Me."

Later that summer, I did what my Fuller Pool advisor had suggested: I purchased a Levi's denim jacket at Bargain Days. How could I not? And I paid a little more money to get one without any defects. I did continue to wear somewhat defective clothing at times. However, I shed the odd orange socks that summer.

Just to make life a little easier.

CHAPTER 25
October 1972

Sharp Scissors and a Bunsen Burner

THE DOWNSIDE OF SO MUCH FREEDOM in Ann Arbor in the 1960s and 1970s was that things often spun out of control, particularly within the walls of the schools. Marvin Gaye's "What's Going On" was an apt theme for that time, both for Ann Arbor as a whole and for how I felt navigating junior high.

What was going on was that I did not like disorder, and yet, from 1971 to 1973, I found myself in the chaotic halls of Slauson Junior High. And while I enjoyed my time there immensely, the school never seemed entirely safe to me. And it was filled with disorder. There were empty stairways to nowhere. Not enough teachers in the hallways. Smoking in the bathrooms. A menacing boys' locker room with rusted lockers and decrepit shower areas. The auditorium and balcony were open during the day, and there were always problems there. More weird stairs behind the auditorium. An empty room above the balcony. Big band lockers that people got pushed into. Bullying, at times, and strife.

And the rumors of other problems circulated: A kid taking a shot-gun to Forsythe Junior High. A stabbing at Tappan Junior High. Fights in the high schools and other junior highs. And a sure sign of the decline of civilization to me: girls fought in the hallways.

Despite this, I liked many of the dedicated teachers and found kind and talented classmates to spend time with. I did make some enemies, and I had to watch my back at times. Mainly because I had a tendency to try and tell classmates what to do. I scuffled at times, but I also became fairly adept at reading social situations and defusing conflicts. I did this by getting to know as many people as possible. And in the end, I could always run away fast from a tricky situation if need be.

Some of the turmoil came from the racial strife that trickled down from the high schools. Some thought that this discord was part of the wave of riots in the nation's cities, including the 1967 Detroit riots, and white flight from Detroit. The Ann Arbor Public Schools had been dealing with this conflict in the 1970–71 school year. There were fights among students at Pioneer High School, and the Pioneer library had been damaged in October 1970. Human relations counselors were assigned to the schools and roamed the hallways, working to create community and de-escalate tensions.

As much as I loved Ann Arbor, it was clear that there was racism here, as there was everywhere. In a self-proclaimed progressive town, I learned that even the first Black mayor of Ann Arbor, Albert Wheeler—who lived next door to Slauson—had difficulty getting a mortgage for a home in that area because of illegal redlining.

A stark lesson in insidious racism confronted me in the Slauson library in the fall of 1972 in eighth grade. I watched a kid I knew take a very large pair of scissors from a table and put it under his jacket. I was sitting right next to him. I asked him what he was doing with that pair of scissors. He said he may need it for protection. He said his cousin from Pioneer had been beaten up by some Black kids after that cousin had been with some white kids who had beaten up some other Black kids. It was a little hard to follow. He said he was now going to join his cousin and a group that evidently was going to further retaliate by picking on some random Black kid from Slauson after school that day.

"I'm going to join this NBC," he said about the group he was going to join.

I was stunned when he told me what this stood for, and then I moved close to him and took the scissors from him. "I'd rather stab you in the heart right now than have you join this club," I was surprised to hear myself say.

I gave the scissors to the librarian and told her I didn't think this was a very good item to leave out around young people and rolled my eyes over to my classmate. I told my classmate that I was going to tell the principal about this disturbing club.

So I went to the principal, Collier E. Owens, a kind, quiet, and dignified Black man with a very thin mustache. I told him what I had learned. He asked me what I thought of all this. "This is not good," was all I could respond.

And after that, I became a confidential informant for the principal. For a number of policy reasons and practical reasons, I only provided information concerning physical violence: who threw the first punch, etc. Other things, such as cheating or possession of contraband of some sort, I often observed, but I couldn't spend all day snitching about these things.

In any case, my classmate who initially had the scissors got hauled down to the principal's office. He saw me after school and told me he was going to let people know that I was a snitch. I gave him a response that I had learned, over time, worked quite well to calm things down as long as it was given with proper intonation: "No. You are not going to do that."

The next time I saw the principal, he warned me about threats concerning scissors and bodily harm. I assured him it was said just for effect.

"Don't do that," he explained, "it just spirals out of control."

The next time I had an opportunity to talk with the principal was about an incident involving a Bunsen burner. In Mr. Mastie's science class, we were working on something called a "Sludge Project." We were given an amount of unidentified material and had to perform various tests to determine what it was composed of.

This project was, perhaps, a metaphor for junior high itself: What am I?

Some of the tests involved a Bunsen burner—something that should never be allowed in a junior high school. My lab partner, a friend, was holding up the Bunsen burner, and I backed into it with my long hair flying around. Now, hair doesn't really burn; it just singes upward. And the flame took out a big chunk of my hair. Frightened by it, I turned and pushed my hand toward my classmate. Now, this action likely looked like a punch to many people, although it was more of push, and a blow never actually landed. Nevertheless, my friend moved backwards, slipped on something, and hit his head on the hard lab table.

The teacher rushed over and walked him to the office to be looked at. I told the teacher it wasn't really my friend's fault about the Bunsen burner and my hair. My friend even assured the teacher that I had not punched him but that he had slipped. This incident further sealed a bond between us. But he was still led down to the office to be examined.

When the teacher returned, he still sent me down to the counselor's office because my hair stank. Fortunately, as I was walking there, I saw the principal and began to explain why I was in the hall and what was going on. He invited me down to his office. As I sat with him, he made it clear that nothing was going to happen to me because I hadn't actually hit anyone and that it seemed to him that I had acted in response to the Bunsen burner.

"But consider this," I countered, "the class believes that I threw a punch." And there was an injury.

I told him that he might consider sending a strong signal against violence by suspending me. I also reminded him about the information I had provided him in the past. There were some students who still resented the fact that I had provided accurate information to him.

"A suspension might provide me some cover," I explained. I also took the time to ask him an unrelated question I had about Maxey Boys Training School, a juvenile detention facility.

The principal said he wasn't going to suspend me but that he could let me go home if I needed to address my hair.

"Mr. Owens, my hair stinks, and a bunch of it is gone, I have to do something," I said.

Then I pressed him on one procedural point. "No one would have to know that the hair was the reason, correct?" And I clarified with him that my parents would have to pick me up, just like what would happen if this were a suspension.

Mr. Owens stroked his thin mustache and said, "You've got this all thought through haven't you."

My dad came to pick me up and, as we walked out, reflexively put his arm on my shoulder. Principal Owens happened to be outside, in front, talking to someone at a distance and pointing away from the school.

But from the view of any kid in the school looking out the window, particularly all my classmates in the big choir room that looked out over the central sidewalk, it looked like Mr. Owens was pointing for me to leave school grounds. Just like the archangel booting Adam out of the Garden of Eden. And further, from a distance, it looked like my father was leading me out by the scruff of my neck.

Word got out about this incident: Someone was injured. I was escorted home, Principal Owens pointing the way.

I couldn't believe how this was all playing out.

This faux suspension proved to be useful in deterring future altercations. When challenged in the stairway one day, I said I couldn't fight because I had been in a prior altercation, someone was injured, and Principal Owens had spoken to me about Maxey Boys Training School. Now, in carefully stringing these things together, it did create a certain impression.

My potential enemy that day was actually deterred by this recitation of events. "Alright," he said, "that was after your hair got lit on fire by a Bunsen burner, right?"

"Exactly," I said, "it is difficult to control myself when I get riled up."

"And we don't want to get sent to Maxey Boys," the kid said.

I nodded.

I walked away without incident, down the empty stairway and back to class.

"What's going on," Marvin Gaye sang.

Always something at Slauson that year.

In a strange twist of providential fate, this bond with my friend from the Bunsen burner incident saved me from serious injury later in life. In tenth grade, some trouble came walking down B hall, where my locker was at Pioneer High School. I heard a commotion behind me. I saw my friend holding on to a baseball bat that someone else was holding raised in the air. I chuckled as I watched him easily take the bat away from the other kid and order him to walk away in a torrent of words, only some of which I heard. My friend was very tall now and had huge hands.

The kid walking away was someone I had had an altercation with in a stairwell three years earlier at Slauson. He had always threatened to get back at me, but it had never happened. My friend looked at me and warned that I needed to be more aware of my surroundings.

"He was about to bust you on the side of the head with that bat." My friend assured me, though, that I would never need to worry about that kid again. "It's just done, he will never come near you again, believe me."

This was one of the times that I just did not need to know all the details of what my friend had done or had said.

And it was very good to have a friend who truly had my back.

CHAPTER 26
Fall 1972

Open Gym Night at Dicken School

GOING INTO EIGHTH GRADE, I was under the impression that society was in a free fall of turmoil, and my main source for this opinion was my neighbor, Ann Arbor Police Officer Fleming, badge 12. He was a beat cop downtown and on campus, and he knew everyone. He warned my brother and me about everything, from campus riots to fights in the Pioneer High School smoking lounge. (Yes, the school administration tried to regulate underage smoking by allowing it in one cafeteria, a decision soon regretted.)

Officer Fleming had every tool carefully hung up on the wall of his workshop. When I watched him work on a motorcycle or car in his garage, he lectured on the importance of usefulness.

I seemed to be doing my part regarding usefulness, so I thought. In addition to providing math tutoring and helping my older brother with janitorial work, my primary contribution to social usefulness during this time was to deliver the weekly *Huron Valley Ad-Visor* (a shopper with some articles and photos) in a timely manner to over three hundred homes in the Dicken neighborhood. Because of this, I had weekly glimpses into the houses, activities, and families in this neighborhood on my route.

I carefully kept a notebook keeping tabs on whether families paid for their papers, any tips they had given me, and most importantly, whether they had any dogs. The day before Thanksgiving that year, I barely evaded a large, hostile mixed-breed on Tudor Drive while finishing my paper route. Yet, I forgot about the dog as I ran home and began thinking about all the possible doors into Dicken school.

Because later that night, I would head over to Dicken school to shoot baskets inside the gym. I called it "open gym night," which, to my parents, would have implied a school-sanctioned activity. What it actually meant was finding an open door somewhere in the school after the janitor left and playing alone or with friends in the still, clandestine air of an empty gym.

During this time period, most kids had a broad view of public property, and kids in every neighborhood in the city were sneaking into local schools regularly to play basketball. I was obsessed with basketball and played whenever I could, even outside in the cold and rain. I tried to shoot fifty free throws a day in our driveway. During the winter, I played on school teams and in empty school gyms. The great thing about the small Dicken school gym was that you could pass the ball to yourself using the wall because the wall was so close to the out-of-bounds line. Pass. Shoot. Score. The echo of dribbling and shooting cut through the solitude of an empty school. I felt alive. It was sheer joy.

And it was therapy. As I recall, there were three things bothering me that night before Thanksgiving. First, while taking turnaround jumpers from the baseline, I thought about a lesson I had learned the prior week while doing some math tutoring: Never, under any circumstance, provide an opinion during an argument between an eighth-grade classmate and her mother. Even if asked. Particularly if it involves the propriety of singing "The House of the Rising Sun" at the Slauson talent show.

I was at a classmate's kitchen table working through various aspects of square roots, eating freshly baked oatmeal cookies, and absorbing illuminating stray crumbs of Slauson Junior High social gossip. At some point, I was asked to weigh in on the point of disagreement about the song. I agreed with her mom. I should have stuck with math advice.

Second, while I worked on left-handed dribbling and layups, I contemplated a continued injustice concerning my paper route. I had worked very hard in a subscription contest for the *Huron Valley Ad-Visor*. I had been repeatedly told at the office on Packard that I had lined up the most paid yearly subscriptions in the city (for a free paper, mind you), and I was hoping to receive the promised free trip to Disney World. However, to avoid paying for the trip, no doubt, the *Ad-Visor* went bankrupt and reemerged as *The Advisor of Washtenaw County*. The dangled promise of the trip was a casualty. Despite this, I was not yet willing to abandon the route. It gave me an opportunity to keep tabs on things.

Third, while heaving half-court hook shots, I realized that I was never going to get back a 45 record I had lent. It was The Beatles' *Let It Be*. I had lent it to a person who was living in the basement of my father's chapel and had recently skipped town with it, and I was having trouble letting this go—or letting it be.

One of my half-court shots was so far off that it careened through an open gym door and into the hall. Given the holiday season, there were large posters and displays out in the hall, including a thirty-foot collage, with seemingly every stereotypical Thanksgiving scene, on brown butcher paper. It was done by a first-grade class. It also had some ears of dried corn precariously affixed to it.

Other than being thirteen, I don't know what possessed me to throw the basketball against the wall just above the poster where the maize was. The wall vibrated; the corn fell; and in falling, tore the paper from top to bottom. This caused a cascading effect where some of the tape loosened and about ten feet of the cornucopia collage was left hanging off the wall.

I did not panic, exactly, but I knew that I needed some supplies to correct this and headed to the office. Its door was held slightly ajar with a rubber doorjamb. The door closed after I moved the doorjamb aside and entered.

I found myself locked in the office. Perhaps I should have been clued in by the sign on the door that said "maintenance," with an arrow pointing at the door handle. Fortunately, the office had a phone and phone book, so I called Officer Fleming. My thought process for choosing him was muddled. As was my voice when he answered the phone.

"Yes, I am trapped in a Dicken school office," I told him.

"Through no fault of my own," I added, explaining how he could get into Dicken through a certain door.

"You better have a good explanation for this," were his last words on the phone.

It seemed like a very long time before he came; I read a school Standard Operating Procedures manual while I waited. When Officer Fleming peered at me through the office's window and tapped on the glass, I felt like a zoo animal about to be released.

He came prepared—with a large tool kit. He got the door open quickly and, always handy, also fixed the doorknob problem. We then worked together to put the Thanksgiving collage back up, and Office Fleming chewed me out using colorful language, fascinating word combinations, and expressive modulations of tone. He pointed his finger at me, the tip of which I had once held in a glass of milk on the way to the emergency room. I was headed down the path of lawlessness was his gist. Trespassing was a gateway activity in his mind.

But I was most impressed by his artistry: he duct-taped the torn paper in a way that actually fit into the collage quite well, like a tree branch.

He did not give me a ride home that night. He made it clear that he wanted me to consider the consequences of my actions. Walking home in the cold and mist, resolving to never again bounce a ball off a hallway wall near maize on a Thanksgiving display, I took a right onto Waltham. I then would have just a left onto Windsor to go. From there, three houses down, then a cut through Officer Fleming's yard. I would soon be home.

But as I tossed my basketball into the air, I noticed a dark shape on the top of the hill at Mushroom Park, making me nervous. I picked up the pace, looked back, dropped the ball, and sprinted down Windsor. I slipped on the wet grass in Officer Fleming's side yard and fell, waiting to be mauled.

I saw Officer Fleming step from his garage as I went down. I heard a commanding, "Come here." I didn't see exactly what happened, but when I looked back, the menacing dog from Tudor Drive was in Officer's Fleming's thick hands. He was speaking very firmly to the dog, who seemed happy to see Officer Fleming.

"I've caught him many times off leash," he said. "His owners are careless." He led the dog into his garage, then came out with a bit of rope for a leash.

I was directed to take the dog back to its owners. Shaking his head, Officer Fleming lectured: "Never run away from a dog, man. Let me explain something here: always control the situation."

As I walked away with the dog, he added, "I don't want to see you out and about anymore tonight."

The dog owners were grateful and gave me three dollars for my troubles. I walked back through Mushroom Park and admired the two-hundred-year-old white oak tree that had existed long before Ann Arbor.

When I got home, my mom had just brought out Thanksgiving rolls. She asked me to remind her to send a note of appreciation to the principal about open gym night. I would obviously need to carefully lead her away from this kind impulse. My mom also said that a girl had called about math help and had left a number.

The day after Thanksgiving, I went to Discount Records and bought another copy of *Let It Be* with the three dollars from the dog owners. "The House of the Rising Sun" was playing in the background as I went to the cashier. I asked the young woman at the register, who was wearing a *Star Trek* t-shirt, what she thought about the song.

"Why do you want to know?" she inquired.

Since I couldn't really answer that, I just thanked her for the record and left.

Nevertheless, the song reminded me to return the call to my classmate. When I did, she didn't say anything about our prior tutoring session and the "The House of the Rising Sun" dispute.

And neither did I.

CHAPTER 27
March 1973

———

Band and Basketball

ON MARCH 5, 1973, MY FATHER took time from his sermon preparation to draft a document to Slauson Junior High band teacher Daniel Long, a very tall, influential, and excellent teacher. The letter can best be described as a memorandum of understanding that had been brokered between my father and Mr. Long regarding an upcoming band festival that was scheduled on the same day as a basketball tournament. This was a problem.

The "future plans" listed under my picture in the eighth-grade yearbook simply stated "play pro basketball." I did not have any backup plan at that point. This is why the Ann Arbor Recreation Department's Saturday morning eighth-grade basketball was so important. Eight city teams. Two games at different times. We had a coach who had played semi-professional football and knew everything about football—but nothing about basketball. We practiced at the dusty gym of Bach Elementary School while the coach yelled instructions laced with obscenities. He wore a white t-shirt and a red checkered hunting cap at all times. He carried an electrician's knife on his belt. He terrified us into being a strong team. We even got to play an exhibition match at the half-time of a U-M college basketball game. Before a packed arena, I shot an air ball and made a turn-around jump shot from the baseline.

Rec & Ed eighth grade team, 1973. My father, Don Postema, is in the top right, and I am in the front row, wearing the number 2 shirt.

I was a better basketball player than musician.

But being in junior high band provided a great sense of purpose to me. I was always impressed by the musical talents of my classmates. As a drummer, I got to sit and stand in the back of the practice room and watch my classmates perform. Prowling around the percussion section during band practice with my fellow drummers, moving to and from various drums, allowed me to watch Mr. Long control the large collection of students. Mr. Long was a kind and beloved teacher. He had a large sign that said "STUG" on the wall, "guts" spelled backward, which was meant to inspire determination. He also lived up the street from me, and I delivered his newspaper, the *Huron Valley Ad-Visor*.

I had peremptorily told Mr. Long that I would not attend the band festival because of a conflict with basketball on the upcoming Saturday morning. It became clear that Mr. Long was not in agreement with this plan. My father, a skilled manager of conflict and people, went with me to Mr. Long's house and worked out a compromise memorialized in that letter, written on church stationary evidently to solemnize the agreement. It said, in part: "Whereas, Stephen is willing to compromise by coming to the 'performance' part of the festival and missing one basketball game, and then playing the second basketball games and missing the 'sight-reading' portion of the festival. Therefore, Stephen will be excused after the performance of the festival, Saturday, March 10, 1973."

I believe, but have yet to get my father to admit, that when I left the room briefly at Mr. Long's house to get some water offered by his wife, my father stressed that the band might actually be better off without me at the sight-reading portion of the festival, as "it might not be his forte." I heard some of those words but not the whole conversation. Walking home, my father simply said that Mr. Long was a very reasonable man.

The band played well, and we, in the end, received the highest marks. I looked at all of my classmates arrayed in their band uniforms: white pants or skirts, white shirts, and Slauson capes. My parents rushed me over to the tournament after the performance, and I changed in the car. My parents raised an issue that "would be discussed later" so as to not throw off my concentration. We won the basketball game, although my shot was off, as my band-related concern was closing in on me.

Earlier at the festival, I knew immediately that I was in a predicament when I entered the set-up area. I had forgotten to wear the band uniform. I *had* a nice pair of white pants and a white shirt. But they remained in the closet while I had inexplicably put on black pants and a rose-colored shirt. It was quite an uncomfortable situation, and I believe Mr. Long might ordinarily have sent me home if not for the fact that he knew I would then be able to avoid the festival altogether and go to both basketball games, contrary to our carefully crafted settlement agreement.

And this was never my intent. In fact, I was quite embarrassed by the clothing situation. Mr. Long said nothing, and the performance proceeded. I knew I would be talking with Mr. Long later in the day. On the way home from the basketball game, my younger sisters kept asking my parents why I had not worn the correct clothing. There simply was no explanation.

To my father, it was a bad faith breach of an implied condition of the brokered deal memorialized on church stationary. The condition that, in going to the performance part of the festival, I would be in uniform. To my mother, a schoolteacher, it was a breach of decorum, rude to my classmates, and it tarnished the family name. My brother just laughed when he heard about it.

My mom insisted that I spend the afternoon crafting a written apology, and she had to approve the form and content. I went through several drafts. I worked in my father's study while he was working on a Sunday sermon. The pictures of Martin Luther King Jr. in the study looked down on me.

The apology was several paragraphs long and incorporated educational, psychological, and theological themes and terms. After getting my mother's approval, I was on my own to deal with Mr. Long, a very kind man that I had wronged. Not totally alone, as I did bring my English springer spaniel Duke along for moral support in my walk over to Mr. Long's house to deliver my letter.

He was gracious yet firm at the same time. I did not have to go into his house, which, frankly, was part of the reason why I brought my dog along.

When I got home, I was grounded; my mom said that I should probably stay in for the rest of the day. The weather wasn't good anyway, so it was not a real hardship. My punishment was confinement for a period of time in my father's study. The study with his thousands of books that I could read in the excellent large leather chair—a favorite activity. My mother had supervised the drafts of the apology letter. But she also provided mercy in the form of apple bread.

Sitting in the chair that day in March, I felt like a burden had lifted. I had messed up, no doubt. But I knew that, come Monday, I would be back in band class to face the comments of my classmates, and that, too, could be weathered.

"Don't cause a band uniform problem" became a saying that everyone in our family understood.

CHAPTER 28
August 1973

First Cross-Country Practice

THE TWO-HUNDRED-ACRE Pioneer High School campus and adjacent Greenview and Pioneer Woods Nature Area were one mile from our house down Scio Church Road. The track and the cross-country running paths of this campus became a major part of my life in high school.

It was at the track in August of 1973 that I first met Coach Don Sleeman, then in his sixth year of coaching. All ninth graders had been moved from Slauson Junior High to Pioneer High School, and I was one of only two freshmen that joined the cross-country team.

I made my first mistake that day by taking the advice of an older neighbor boy who encouraged me to immediately let the coach know of my motivation by declaring that I was there to join the varsity cross-country team. So, in front of all the runners on the team, I went up to the coach and did just that.

Without looking up from his clipboard, Coach Sleeman said, "Well, that's not really how it works here."

The next things Coach Sleeman barked at me were, "Don't come back. With those shoes. Athletic Department voucher. Stein & Goetz Sporting Goods."

My mother had recently found my shoes at State Street Bargain Days for less than a dollar. They were some sort of knockoff that had been made to look like Adidas with similar striping, but it had little tread. I was wearing them for the first time that morning. They caused me to slip on the dew-covered grass.

I kept up with the seniors the whole way, running along what I would soon learn was the team's mile-long warmup jog, which ended back at the track for stretching. I thought, how hard could cross-country be? Even with my slippery new shoes, I had kept up with everyone on the run.

My second mistake that morning was thinking that the practice was over after that preliminary jog. As I started to leave, Coach Slee-man growled, "Where do you think you're going?"

He then turned us loose in groups to run all over town. I was not in the varsity group but with the newcomers. I limped back to the track with blisters at the end of a several-mile run. Coach shook his head when looking at my shoes. His final reminder, "Shoes. Voucher. Today."

When I got home, I didn't have the heart to tell my mother how terrible the bargain shoes were. Instead, I told her that we were all required to have matching shoes. So, that afternoon, I got a pair of Adidas Country running shoes, white with green stripes. The school voucher covered all but $2 of the cost of the shoes, which were $9.99. For just $2, I began what would be the most important activity for me at Pioneer from 1973 to 1977.

I clearly had provided some amusement for the team that morning, a team that would place second in the state that year and then first in the unofficial national meet. Two members of the team placed ninth and tenth in the state meet, and after I watched that race, I vowed to do as well as or better in my career. Despite my naiveté—and some other crazy things I did that year—the team was kind and encouraging to me.

Over those years, the long-distance runners on the cross-country and track teams trained an absurd amount in every type of weather. We ran in packs—sometimes only in shorts and sometimes in soggy sweats. We baked and we froze. We laughed and cursed. We praised and complained about our demanding coach. Sometimes we ran on a dirt road—Coach would track us down in his banana-yellow station wagon and tell us to pick up the pace. The back window of his car had obscenities written in the caked-on dirt.

In the summer of 1976, I even got a city map and made it a point to run on every street in the city.

Me racing, Fall 1976.

I learned how important the great music of the day was to keep me company on our long runs. Just singing in my mind gave me energy. Pumped me up. Any song with good beat or words. We ran west and south on dusty dirt roads, past menacing farm dogs: Scio Church, Tessmer, Waters Road, Ellsworth, Lohr. Bruce Springsteen's "Born to Run" and George Harrison's "What Is Life" carried me through. We ran east to the hill in the Arboretum and onto Gallup Park. Creedance Clearwater Revival's "Have You Ever Seen the Rain" or "Bad Moon Rising"—really anything by CCR—played in my mind. We ran through the Diag on campus, and I might have been humming "Magic Carpet Ride" by Steppenwolf.

And, yes, when traffic was light, we sometimes ran down the centerline on Main Street because, well, because we were alive and young. Bachman–Turner Overdrive's "Takin' Care of Business" carried me down Main Street back to Pioneer.

And we felt strong. I heard Bob Seger in concert years later describe being on the cross-country team at Ann Arbor High School in the 1960s and getting back from a summer practice run on those same roads. That was his inspiration for lyrics in his song "Like a Rock": standing, sweating in the sun after practice in the height of summer, feeling strong.

And he was right.
Our strong and sure strides embraced the city.
Running around town, Ann Arbor was ours.

CHAPTER 29
Thanksgiving 1973

The List

I GAVE MY CONFIDANTE THE LIST five days after Thanksgiving, three days after the wet Saturday of the Michigan football game against Ohio State. Both teams were undefeated going into the game. Ohio State was ranked number one in the nation and Michigan number four. The game ended in a ten-to-ten tie that was unsatisfactory to everyone involved. Michigan's quarterback broke his collarbone. The Michigan kicker missed two field goals at the end of the game, including one with only seconds left.

I felt bad for both of them.

And I was also feeling a little sorry for myself. I had bought tickets to the game earlier in the week in front of the Michigan Union, then sold them that morning near the stadium for a little less than what I had paid. I had developed a good sense for ticket reselling that fall, but that day, I was just off my game. And I learned a year later that ticket resale was actually frowned upon by the authorities.

The unsatisfactory tie game and coming up short in the rain caused me to seek solace, that night, from two reliable sources: math and music. I began working on geometry in my room, listening to our stereo, which had good reception and speakers. Geometry homework was a priority, as I especially liked my class at Pioneer High with Mr. Larson. Because of him, I became passionate about geometry, for all of its symmetries, shapes, and elegant patterns.

The music bounced off the lime-green walls and the black-and-white tile floor of my room, which was half below ground, bringing different worlds into my room. And the music was sublime: The Big 8, CKLW AM 800, and rock on WRIF. And two stations that played a lot of soul music and R & B and were close together near 1400 on the "AM" dial: WJIB and WCHB.

That night, I was listening so intently to a radio program that my focus wandered from the beauty of geometry to the allure of romance. And how could it not? The singers transcended time and place: Aretha Franklin (the Queen of Soul), Stevie Wonder, Al Green, Barry White, Percy Sledge, Sam Cooke (the King of Soul). Then the song "Love Train" by The O'Jays came on, one of the best dance songs of the 1970s. While it was more generally about universal love and harmony in the world, it provided overwhelming encouragement for me to get on board the love train.

As fast as possible.

I was tapping my pencil to the beat, and the next thing I knew, I found myself writing out a list of qualities and characteristics that I thought would be necessary, almost as Euclidean axioms, and would lead deductively to a girlfriend.

I was methodical about this, creating a ranked list of the basics. The first quality on the list was mathematical interest. I enjoyed my geometry class and wanted someone I could regularly talk with about the beauty of math. At age fourteen, the rest of the list flowed logically for me:

2) *Knowledgeable about basketball and other sports (my passion. A true appreciation of the 1973 college basketball finals or NBA finals would be great)*

3) *Likes the TV shows M*A*S*H and Kung Fu*

4) *Likes to read (interest in prison escape books a plus)*

5) *Enjoys Motown music and current events (I had been captivated by the music variety show Soul Train and the Senate Watergate hearings during the past year)*

6) Likes to run or bike around the city

7) Mature

8) Has excellent handwriting

9) Likes to bake

10) No perfume (allergic)

While I was lacking a girlfriend in the traditional sense, I was fortunate that two of my good friends and confidantes were young women whom I had met at Slauson. They lived nearby, and I spent time with each of them discussing the state of life in junior high and high school. They were fountains of useful social information to me. They also had boyfriends at times, so I believed they could help me efficiently cut through the convoluted social processes of obtaining a girlfriend.

I had witnessed one of them do a great act of kindness early on in seventh grade, when I barely knew her. After she walked away, someone made fun of her for this kindness, and to my surprise, I found myself telling the person to stop talking about my very good friend. Word got back to her about this.

"Hey, I hear we are friends," she said the next day.

"Yes. Or else I will be a liar," I explained.

"Okay then."

And after that, I began stopping over at her house on the way home from Slauson and Pioneer, cutting through her backyard. We often chatted on her front porch. She was a valuable advisor.

That week after the Thanksgiving holiday, the day the United States Senate voted to confirm Congressman Gerald Ford from Michigan as vice president by a vote of 95 to 3, I decided to bring the list over to my confidante for her take on it.

Frankly, as well as I knew her, I couldn't quite read her eyes or facial expressions as she took an initial glance at the list and looked back at me and then back at the list. Her next words were that we really needed to sit down.

Running by fast down on Main Street. With permission of Ken Cobb, Ann Arbor photographer.

My friend asked me what had actually prompted the handwritten list. "Well, do you want to know the truth?" I asked. I told her about doing geometry, being mesmerized by soul music.

"And then 'Love Train' came on. And that was that."

"Really? Okay. I won't tell anyone about this process," she assured me.

She then analyzed the list out loud, asking questions such as, "Is this in order of importance? Does math have to be the very first on the list?" And, "Mature? Trust me on this, it could be really misconstrued."

And so on.

"Okay, now number eight, why 'excellent handwriting' when yours is frantic?" she inquired as she pointed to my scrawls. I felt a little awkward explaining that I envied really excellent cursive writing and that good penmanship was intriguing to me.

She looked me in the eyes and said, "The truth now. You just find good cursive writing really attractive, don't you?"

I was fourteen; what could I say? I did actually imagine beautiful notes in beautiful cursive from a girlfriend that I did not have yet.

She continued: "Now back to three. *M*A*S*H* is good, but *Kung Fu* on this list, let's think this through."

"*Kung Fu* is a very historical and philosophical show," I pointed out. Plus, the fighting was quite inspiring. (I didn't tell her about the havoc that ensued in our den during the attempted re-creations of those fight scenes with my brother during the commercials.)

She just shook her head and imitated Master Po, the Shaolin priest, "How is it you do not understand?" Her comment itself demonstrated the broad social relevance of the show. But I agreed to delete it.

"Anything else to add?"

"Maybe someone who has things she is really passionate about that I do not know anything about," I said.

"All right now," she agreed, "that is a very good one."

I went on: "It would be great if she had a really excellent stamp collection?"

"Hmm, let's stop while you're ahead here." That, evidently, was a little too specific for her.

She got a pen and paper, and we redid the list together. She made some suggestions concerning things I may have missed, helped reorder the priorities, and then wrote it out—in excellent handwriting.

Girlfriend List

1) Friendly and enjoys school

2) Likes reading and math

3) Kind

4) Likes Motown music and current events

5) Interested in or good at something I know nothing about

6) Self-confident (and no perfume)

7) Likes to run or bike around the city

8) Extra credit for interest or ability: sports (basketball in particular), M*A*S*H, penmanship, and baking.

She said this list was now a little more flexible. "Remember that you are looking for an actual person."

"Yes, yes." I admitted that it was all still pretty theoretical at this point. Just a list on paper, after all.

She said she would think about this over the next couple of weeks and we could meet later and discuss possible options. I knew that she was attuned to the inner workings of Pioneer High School much better than I was. Frankly, I trusted her, and I was actually hoping she could just pick out someone for me and arrange the whole thing.

One last thing: she said that I might want to focus on prospects in my math class. I had thought of that too. My geometry class had many interesting people. They were also pretty intense. Some wore wire-rimmed glasses, others toted Kurt Vonnegut books. Many carried stringed instruments. A couple of them told me, in hushed but excited tones, about something called the "Michigan Mathematics Prize Competition," saying that I might be interested in it. However, I didn't know many of them, as I was one of the few ninth graders in that class. Despite this, they were kind to me.

I had enjoyed sitting next to one of the young women in the class, who seemed to be enjoying everything about geometry. I also seriously envied her new HP-45 scientific calculator (with a revolutionary shift key), which had just come out over the summer. And as far as I could observe, she also had at least two Scripto mechanical pencils and an endless supply of 0.7 mm pencil lead.

She slipped me a note one day that said: "Don't you love this class? Mr. Larson is cool." She was wearing a black dress with small colorful fruit printed on it. It looked like a black light poster from Middle Earth. I stared at the note and her excellent handwriting for the rest of class as if I had been wandering in the wilderness and the note in my hand was manna from heaven.

I saw my confidante later that week in the hall outside the Pioneer library. As always, we had things to talk about. I told her I was actually making some progress on the project we had discussed. I showed her the note.

"Wow. That is some sweet cursive," she said.

"Yeah, she is in my geometry class and friendly. She also has a really amazing new calculator. Also, get this: her favorite TV show is *Kung Fu*," I paused. "Well, just kidding. About the show. Not the calculator."

I told my confidante that I was thinking about asking the note writer out sometime but just hadn't found the right time or words yet.

"The note is a good sign," she said.

So, I asked the note writer out.

Having a kind, interesting, and older girlfriend made ninth grade pass quickly. We were also in biology class together and dissected a perch, a frog, a pig's heart, and other things together. The fact that her family had a drum set in their living room and a pinball machine in their basement was a bonus.

The next thing I knew, we were walking down Stadium Blvd., and she was telling me she was going up north to her family's cottage for the summer. We were walking from Pioneer High to the new Ponderosa Steak House on a very hot, humid Saturday night, near the end of the semester. We had steak dinners that cost $1.99—drinks and dessert were extra. Why I was wearing a long-sleeved polyester shirt with a large collar that night remains a mystery. It stuck to my skin in very odd ways.

She left for the summer. But she let me borrow her calculator while she was gone, as she knew there were some functions via the shift key that I wanted to explore further. We wrote letters to each other. Over time, the letters mentioned a young man that was working near her cottage—a college freshman majoring in math and business, who had a mustache and a car. He was nineteen.

In August, I received my final letter from her just before watching Vice President Ford be sworn in as president of the United States on television. I was happy for President Ford since he was from Michigan and was a friend of our former neighbor Congressman Esch. In fact, I was proud to see Mr. Esch standing next to Ford as he was sworn in.

I was digesting the words in her letter (and a blueberry muffin) as Ford spoke: "This is an hour of history that troubles our minds and hurts our hearts."

I could completely identify with those words, given the letter I had received.

I had to take the letter over (for complete deciphering) to the confidante who had revised the list with me. Notwithstanding the many cushioning phrases, the truth was clear: she was moving on to a new boyfriend—the college math major.

"Yes, this is over for you," my confidante told me after she read the letter.

She patted me on the arm. "But, look, you made a good impression on her for her to take the time to write such a kind and lengthy letter."

She added that a five-month girlfriend is very long for ninth grade.

"She was really good at math, and friendly," I responded.

"I'm sure that this makes it extra difficult," my friend said, empathy in her voice. At that moment—salt in the wound—I realized that I was also going to have to give back her HP-45 calculator.

"You have to move on," my confidante said, giving me the letter back.

We talked about our tenth-grade class schedules and the things she hoped to do in the coming year. I guaranteed that she would enjoy geometry. She guaranteed that the love train would come around for me again. "But not if you sneak *Kung Fu* back on to that list of yours," she joked as I began to get on my bike.

This made me laugh, and I almost tipped over. I thanked her and said I would have to think about the list some more. I was certain that all my running around town during cross-country practices would provide ample time for further reflection.

Despite being abruptly kicked off the love train in the summer of 1974, my very kind and wise confidante had put it all in context for me and cheered me up at the same time. "Remember the song that inspired your list," she said. And the words from The O'Jays, which still floated over the nation's airwaves and through Ann Arbor's radio stations, did provide infinite assurance: that the love train would keep on riding on through.

CHAPTER 30
Fall 1974

Meeting a Bibliophile, and a Ticket

SOPHOMORE YEAR AT PIONEER HIGH SCHOOL began just before President Ford pardoned Richard Nixon. My cross-country teammates and I debated this action on the cross-country trails that September. But for all the political craziness in the nation, I was more focused on the social craziness of high school in Ann Arbor.

The Pioneer High School library was usually a place of solitude for me in the midst of the chaos. In the library, I could observe my fellow students carefully from the shadows of the bookshelves and listen to the goings-on. I was lingering near the stacks one warm September afternoon at the beginning of tenth grade. Nearby, a group of classmates were discussing Dickens' *Great Expectations*. Many of these young women I had not yet met, as they came from another junior high. They were bright and talkative, and many were daughters of University of Michigan professors.

I had read the book, so it was clear that one of the young women was particularly knowledgeable about it. She looked straight at me and asked, "Did you learn anything in particular listening to us?"

I couldn't deny that I had been eavesdropping. I was somewhat tongue-tied and said that it seemed that she had read the book very carefully. She looked puzzled, as if wondering if there were any other way to read a book.

This young woman was barefoot, which I found surprising. I also took note that she was carrying Ken Kesey's *One Flew Over the Cuckoo's Nest*. A mutual friend then introduced us. After the barefoot classmate left, I asked the mutual friend about her and was told that this classmate was a free spirit who loved singing and books. I mused aloud that maybe I would get a chance to talk to her further about the book she was carrying.

Then came the social reality of high school in the form of a voice from another classmate nearby. Like fingernails across a blackboard, she asked, "But really now, you wouldn't have anything to say to her. Would you?"

I looked at this provocateur and laughed. I should have left it at that, but I made the mistake of pressing her: "Why would that be?"

"Well, she is a bibliophile. And you. You just ... just run excessively."

Since, at that moment, I didn't know exactly what a bibliophile was, all I could say in my defense was that I was on the cross-country team.

I surmised that a bibliophile might be a member of a Bible-based religious sect where they weren't supposed to talk with outsiders—and where, perhaps, they didn't wear shoes—but I didn't want to display my ignorance. So I said nothing further. When the provocateur walked away, the mutual friend rolled her eyes after her while I went to the nearby dictionary and looked up the word "bibliophile."

After cross-country practice that day, I stopped over at my confidante's house on the way home. She had helped me with my girlfriend list in ninth grade, and I had to tell her about this interaction: that some girl in the library opined that I would have nothing to say to a classmate who was a booklover.

"She was in my business," I said, "maybe because she was high."

The Pioneer Woods across the street from Pioneer's South Seventh entrance was often filled with marijuana smokers. The city, earlier that year, had reenacted the five-dollar pot law, a minimal fine for those in possession. With or without this law, pot was everywhere in the city—even in some elementary schools—and had been for a long time.

Or, my confidante suggested, this provocateur was simply one of those mean girls who liked to mess with people.

As to running, this mean girl didn't know what she was missing.

At sixteen, I would likely have exploded if I did not run every day. My confidante said she was even thinking of joining the track team in the spring. She was glad to hear I was doing well on the varsity cross-country team. I told her the secret reason for my improvement was that I had many good psych-up songs that were helping me run faster.

My top song that season started with a stunning guitar riff followed by a really strong drum beat: "Up Around the Bend" by Creedence Clearwater Revival. If any song could capture the passion of running cross-country, this was it, with its description of running towards a place up ahead, as fast as one could run.

"That is a good song," she agreed.

It was energetic, and it provided focus and energy with words about pondering perpetual motion. This was a song that could help anyone run.

She wanted to know if I actually sang while I was racing.

"More like humming, sometimes some mumbling."

She said she would keep that in mind.

One day later that fall, after cross-country season, I was listening to that exact song and waiting for my brother to come home to help me with some math analysis. My brother wasn't a runner, but he was a serious singer and a better student than I. Better, in part, because he was more precise and actually completed all of his work in a timely manner. He was also really into classical and choral music. He was the president of Pioneer's a cappella choir, and he sang in the University of Michigan Choral Union, a community choir that had been singing Handel's *Messiah* in Ann Arbor every year since 1876.

He had been driving home from the *Messiah* rehearsal that Monday night before Thanksgiving. When he came home, he was quite agitated. He explained that he was making a left turn from Stadium onto Main Street, and out of nowhere, a police car with sirens had come up behind him. The officer claimed my brother had gone through a red light. He was given a ticket.

My brother explained that the officer had claimed to see the red light in his rearview mirror—not directly but reflecting off a puddle in the road. The officer pointed out where his police car had been located. My brother was the wrong person to give such a specific explanation to.

Before he went home, he made some rough drawings and calculations on the back of his *Messiah* score.

Several weeks later, my father took my brother, dressed in a corduroy sport coat, to the 15th Judicial District Court to contest his ticket. He brought along his physics textbook. I suggested that I should go along as a character witness to attest that my brother was an excellent driver and could not be distracted. In fact, my brother was, as the basses sang in the *Messiah*, incorruptible.

And I suggested that I could explain to the judge how focused my brother was. I had driven with my brother once, and on the drive, he picked up two friends and then dropped them off near campus. One of the young women who got in the car was angry at her mom for making her wear a bra. Through the rearview mirror, I could tell she was doing something under her shirt. She proceeded to take her bra off under her shirt in a Houdini-like maneuver. She held it up and said she would burn it on the Diag at the appropriate time.

My mind couldn't quite wrap itself around the geometry of this maneuver, but my brother calmly paid close attention to the road. He never even looked back in the mirror—even with the bra being waved in the air. The young woman was exasperated. "I shouldn't have to wear this, should I?"

Because no one was responding, I piped up saying that I fully agreed with her. I added that it might be difficult to burn a bra without soaking it in some gasoline first.

"Was I talking to you?" she responded. When we got home later, my brother explained what a rhetorical question was and that answering a rhetorical question was neither prudent nor necessary. Particularly if about a bra.

My brother shook his head after hearing my proposed testimony and said that this would be too distracting for the judge and that he would rely solely on the science he had on his side.

My dad described the court scene that night at the dinner table. After the police had gone through their story, my brother made a rough diagram for the judge, showing the mirror, the puddle, and the light. With references from his physics book's chapter on optics, he went on to demonstrate that it was mathematically impossible, because of the angles, for the officer to have seen light from that traffic light in a puddle by way of a rearview mirror. The judge took the matter under advisement and was going to issue a written order. My father and brother were confident of victory.

The court order came in the mail a couple of weeks later. My brother was outraged. The judge had entered a verdict of guilty, claiming that the judge accepted the police testimony. But here is where it got interesting. Rather than impose the usual punishment, the order stated: "However, *under the extenuating circumstances*, the Court suspends all fines and costs in this matter."

The only extenuating circumstances that existed were that the police were not telling the truth. I showed the order to our next-door neighbor Officer Fleming. He agreed that the judge actually believed my brother and should have done the right thing by just declaring him innocent. My brother wanted to appeal the order, but there was no appeal in such a civil infraction.

But I got to thinking about another solution. I thought about President Ford's pardon of Nixon. This blanket pardon bothered me, as I had followed the Watergate hearings carefully. If President Ford could pardon a clearly guilty ex-president from serious crimes, perhaps he could wipe away the guilty verdict of an innocent person entirely.

I even offered to draft a pardon request for my brother. "Remember," I reminded my brother, "then-Congressman Ford wrote our father in 1960 and said if there was anything he could to assist my father, please contact him at any time. Well, now is clearly the time.

"This offer will surely apply to other members of the family," I went on. "We are the former neighbors of Ford's good friend Congressman Marvin Esch. And this miscarriage of justice took place in the shadow of the Michigan Stadium, where Ford had been an all-American."

Finally, I suggested a religious appeal: it had happened on the way home from a *Messiah* rehearsal, of all things.

Plus, my brother had already been planning to write the White House to get a signed picture of the president for his autograph collection, so the pardon request could just be attached. But my brother rejected my scheme. My brother was innocent and did not want a pardon, as he felt they were for the guilty. And he simply did not want to be in the same category as Nixon. Some months later, my brother did, in fact, receive a large envelope from the White House. It was an eight-by-ten glossy photograph of the president with a note written on it: "With best wishes, Gerald R. Ford."

Looking back at 1974, we had a new president—educated at the University of Michigan. I had learned what the word bibliophile meant. I learned what a rhetorical question was. I had a smart brother, who had a keen understanding of science and had a mustache. He had fought the law and had at least won a moral victory.

And the best thing was that I had a song that year that kept me in perpetual motion, running up around the bend, keeping me energized and focused into the next year.

And the song was perfect.

CHAPTER 31
December 1974

JV Basketball and a Wet Towel

I PARTICULARLY ENJOYED ONE PERK of being on the Pioneer High School junior varsity basketball team: the crusty white towels that were provided every day by unseen staff from the gigantic industrial laundry room near the locker room. The strongly bleached towels were barely absorbent; some had rust stains, and they pushed the water off your skin. But, to me, their scratchiness felt good on itchy skin after a hot shower and long practice in the cold of winter, with its dry air.

There was a ritual to the basketball season. Team tryouts in the first week of November. The chosen roster, with few surprises, posted by the athletic office. The voucher we received for a discount on a new pair of high-top Converse All Star basketball shoes, which we would wear with new tube socks that almost reached the knees. The walk home every day after practice in the dark, cold, and sometimes the snow.

The season was twenty games, mainly on Friday nights. The hardwood floors, squeaking shoes, and cheers from the stands made a lasting impression. Ten games were in other cities, meaning a bus ride to strange gyms with old and dim locker rooms in unfamiliar places—some with exotic names like "River Rouge." The level of animated conversation on the ride home on the yellow school bus depended on whether the game was won or lost. The season ended in March.

I was a starter, wearing number 51 while I was on the JV team and number 50 on varsity the next year. In tenth grade, I was listed as 6'2" and 170 pounds in the program. But any view of me in the locker room or on the court would make it clear I was at most 160 pounds. I had just come off the many miles of cross-country season. I even ran wind sprints after cross-country practice in anticipation of basketball season, which irritated my cross-country coach because he didn't want me to play basketball. I was rail thin. But I had very sharp elbows.

I was never the fastest person on the court, but I did have a great deal of stamina. I lived for the game and the struggle for rebounds and loose balls and the rather ugly shots that I put up—garbage buckets, they were called. But they often went in—not a swish but a rattling around the rim before finally dropping in. No one would say I had a sweet shot or clever dribble or that I was smooth. My teammates might have used the term "frenetic," if it was a word they had known. And they would acknowledge that I was seriously competitive. I guarded opponents with a severe intensity and without any regard for their personal space. My opponents sometimes called me a "MF" and, sometimes, other related terms. I took this all in stride.

That season, we had just had a hard practice after winning our first three games of the JV season. I was taking off my shoes in the locker room, and I got hit by a soggy towel by someone just screwing around. I paused for a moment to reflect on what my basketball hero for the past nine years would have done in this situation.

The hero: Cazzie Russell.

He was the biggest sports legend in Ann Arbor in the 1960s. Even compared to any Michigan football player during this time, Cazzie was THE star athlete of Ann Arbor. By his senior year, he was the best college basketball player in the nation. He inspired many elementary, junior high, and high school basketball players, who all had a famous picture of Cazzie—wearing number 33, dribbling a basketball—pinned to their wall.

In 1965, when I was almost six, my father had first taken me to see a Michigan basketball game at Yost Field House, an old venue that was cavernous and already forty years old by the time I entered it. It was the largest indoor athletic structure in the United States when it was built in 1923.

Cazzie Russell, 1963. Thumbtacked to numerous young fans' bedroom walls. "Cazzie Russell, UM Men's Basketball, 1963," BL008690, University of Michigan. News and Information Services, env. 3146 fr. 42, Ser B 10, University of Michigan News and Information Services Photographs, Bentley Historical Library, University of Michigan

It was at this game in 1965, just five years old, that I watched Cazzie play for the first time. The venue was from the past, but his game was modern. He played with great purpose and finesse and helped take the Michigan Wolverines basketball team to three Big Ten Conference titles from 1964 to 1966. Crisler Arena, which opened in 1967, was dubbed "The House that Cazzie Built." He was loved in Ann Arbor, and he did student teaching in physical education at Tappan Junior High School. He shot free throws at Yost Field House after practice, and kids would stand silently in line taking turns tossing the balls back. And never talking.

He wrote a book after he graduated from Michigan, and named as the NBA's Number One overall pick, he was drafted by the New York Knicks. His book was called *Me, Cazzie Russell*, and I read its 122 pages many times. I got the book for my eighth birthday. I learned from an article that God had actually told Cazzie to go to Ann Arbor and the University of Michigan.

I was quite impressed by this.

Particularly because, at the time of his decision, he was being recruited by one of the best NBA players in the country, Oscar Robertson—the Big O—to attend the University of Cincinnati, Robertson's alma mater. Robertson had even given Cazzie a pair of his size 14 shoes. But Cazzie called Robertson, turned away his recruitment efforts, and told him that God's purpose was leading him to Ann Arbor. I often wondered what Robertson could have really said in response.

I followed the Michigan team in the paper and watched Cazzie's statistics carefully. I wanted to dribble like him. To shoot like him. Go to the U-M and play basketball and then go to the pros. Just like him.

What I learned from Cazzie's book was that the keys to success in basketball were as follows: Dedication. Work on the fundamentals. Focus on academics (he mentioned prelaw). Do not swear. Be polite. Hum gospel songs. Memorize Bible verses (his top twelve were listed at the end of the book). Be able to run a mile in under six minutes.

So, with this clear roadmap, at eight years old I set out to become a pro basketball player. I was already ahead in the Bible verse category and, eventually, in the running category. I had memory work every day at parochial school, and I knew many Bible verses. I liked gospel hymns already. Did not swear—for the most part. Tried to be polite. Liked school. Had already run a 4:38 mile in track the prior spring.

I took to practicing basketball fundamentals on our driveway whenever I could. I gradually rode to playgrounds and played pickup ball. I attended Pioneer Basketball School in the summer and drilled in the fundamentals further. I played on school teams beginning in sixth grade. I snuck into empty schools and played into the night by myself. I gradually found even more places to play in the city, and by ninth grade, at over six feet tall, I learned how to get into the Intramural Sports Building at U-M and played with college students.

I had prepared for high school basketball for a long time. Despite all my practice, I was simply a pretty good player on the JV team with little likelihood of becoming as good as my heroes. And while Cazzie Russell was always my favorite, I also had another role model in hometown-hero Bob Elliott, the star center of the Pioneer basketball team from 1970 to 1973. I went to the Pioneer games and watched him and the team. He eventually became a star at the University of Arizona and then played in the pros for the New Jersey Nets. He was also a student teacher at Pioneer High School Basketball School in the summer of 1971. He told me I had to learn to shoot and dribble with both hands. He gave me a slight compliment once on a short hook shot, and I then practiced that shot every day.

The Pioneer High School basketball team in Elliott's senior season was ranked number one in the state for most of the season. Pioneer won all twenty of its regular games, then four more in the state playoffs, finally losing in the state quarterfinals to the eventual state champions, Detroit Southwestern. I listened to the game on the radio in my room and was disappointed with the loss.

I worked on the fundamentals, and it had paid off; I was now on a junior varsity basketball team that would end up with a 9–11 record. We'd play in old schools. West on I-94 to Kalamazoo, Battle Creek, Jackson, and Adrian. Up I-23 to Lansing. East on I-94 toward Detroit to play Detroit Pershing, River Rouge, and Highland Park. We'd walk into dusty gyms with strangers watching and letting you know you were not welcome; this gave me the confidence to face difficult situations.

And yet, when I got hit by that towel in the locker room, I did not act with confidence. In the end, even reflecting on Cazzie as a role model, I did not heed the advice that he would have given me: turn the other cheek. Instead, I threw the towel back and hit an innocent bystander. Who then hit me while I was trying to apologize. Teammates broke it up. I called him later that night to apologize.

And we were the closest of friends from that day on, for the rest of high school.

We would sit together on the bus to and from the games. We often lost away games, but we had played. And the reward was having a good friend to talk in hushed tones with on the bus—to talk about everything and nothing. And sometimes we would stop at an isolated McDonald's by a highway exit, with a poorly lit parking lot. Looking out the window of the bus home, there was often a soft beauty to even the urban ugliness seen from the highway. Particularly in the dark and cold and light snow.

Heading back to Ann Arbor.

CHAPTER 32
November 1975

Crashing a Law School Dance

JUNIOR YEAR AT PIONEER. Cross-country season was over. Bruce Springsteen's "Born to Run" had pushed me along this season. I had placed ninth in the state meet. Had I managed to be just ten seconds faster at that meet, I would have placed sixth. Sixth fastest in the state seemed so much better and so attainable. And I couldn't quite let it go, those ten seconds.

Basketball practice would start soon and would help me refocus, and there seemed to be a momentary lull in the press of the year's excessive homework. I was obsessed with the prospect of dunking a basketball. My brother had left for college, and I was facing the abstractions of calculus alone. But it was a worthy pursuit: calculus was about rates of change and forced me to consider the infinite every day.

And Ann Arbor had the perfect laboratory to view change and infinite possibility: the U-M campus. November was the perfect time to roam around the campus on a weekend night with my best friend from the basketball team, looking for things to do and to clear my mind. We didn't want to talk about high school, and we wanted to meet some new people. We headed to the U-M law school, as my friend's mother worked there and he considered it an interesting hangout. We spotted a glow and some activity from inside the beautiful curved window of the Lawyers Club, right near the intersection of State Street and South University.

University of Michigan Law School Quadrangle. With permission of Ken Cobb, Ann Arbor photographer.

The sign at the door said "Law Student Dance Party—No Undergrads." This looked promising to my friend. We were not college undergraduates, he reasoned, so obviously we were permitted to enter. I often deferred to my friend, in part because I was impressed that he took Latin. But I had some hesitation about this interpretation.

I believed that "Law Student" reasonably might also be a requirement. After all, we were in a building devoted to law, and I felt some obligation to look carefully at the context of the sign. I finally rationalized to myself that the sign really wanted those who were students of law (but not undergraduates); I reasoned that one could be a student of the law in the broader sense by being a person interested in the subject of law.

The problem with this rationale was that I didn't meet my own constructed definition, as I had never really been that interested in the law before. I felt that I could remedy the situation by reading up a little bit on the law before I went to the party. With preparation, I could perhaps pass myself off as a law student. And the Law Library across the courtyard provided the perfect solution. I told my friend that I would meet him inside later, after I went to the Law Library to read some law to prepare for the party. He was going straight in, confident he would gain entry with his gift of gab, but he knew me well enough to be tolerant of my rationalizing and other quirks.

I went into the library and immediately took a law book off the shelf to consult. It was volume four hundred of the *Federal Supplement*, which I would learn contained federal district court opinions from across the country. I then flipped through it and landed on a case called the *American East India Corporation v. Ideal Shoe Company*. The title made me chuckle. But it turned out to be a rather dry contract case, difficult to understand. But I did pick up some legal terms that I thought might be useful to throw around at the party, such as "secured transactions," "trover," and "conversion."

I flipped to the middle of the volume, and another case caught my eye: *United States v. Miscellaneous Pornographic Magazines*. Being sixteen, it was the term "miscellaneous" that really set me laughing out loud, disturbing the solemn legal library scene. How could I forget the first line of the case: "The government has brought this case in order to destroy three magazines and a deck of cards ..." Only three magazines? Had the judge looked at each and every card?

This seemed like a lot of federal effort. So I read on.

The judge was quite agitated that these materials violated community standards. The offense was evidently particularly egregious because the items had been sold near the federal courthouse in Chicago. And I did, in fact, go to the end of the opinion to see if, for any reason, some of this obscenity was attached as an exhibit—just to understand the full legal contours of this case. Nothing was attached.

Having briefed myself on contract law and criminal obscenity standards, I felt well prepared to seek entrance to the "Persons Interested in Law Dance Party," as I had mentally renamed it. I certainly felt wiser than when I had entered the Law Library. But I was so focused on gaining entry to the dance that I walked out of the Law Library still carrying volume four hundred of the *Federal Supplement.*

I realized I was still holding the book when the monitor at the party's entrance eyed it as he waved me through.

My friend wasn't in the crowded dining hall area of the party, where I managed to snag a can of Vernors. I found my friend in the Lawyers Club lounge, a beautiful room with tapestries, wood panels, high-back chairs, and portraits of stern lawyers on the walls. He was sitting with three women law students, chatting away. Laughing, he asked how my studies were going. I held up volume four hundred.

I felt compelled, in that moment, to be honest and state the obvious to the women law students: "I'm not actually enrolled in the law school."

"We know that," responded one of the women. Then she softened the blow, "Well, no actual law student would bring a volume of the *Federal Supplement* to a party."

They laughed, but I appreciated the inside information.

A woman from New York wearing a black turtleneck sweater began to cross- examine me in a friendly way: "Is it true that you and your friend, both minors, came here to meet new people? That you did not come here to drink beer, as you both have Vernors? Did you, in fact, as your friend intimated, feel obligated to learn some amount of law to justify your attendance at this law school party?"

I answered in the affirmative to all.

She continued, "Would you young men agree that since you actually made it into the party, you both should actually dance with us awhile so you have something interesting to say about this party back at school?"

I appreciated the utter directness and practicality of her suggestion, her lack of condescension, and her use of the term "young men." As we moved to the dance floor, she also gently suggested that I might want to set volume four hundred down on the couch. And that certainly made good sense.

In the Lawyers Club lounge, near the curved alcove window, my friend and I danced to Motown music with three law students who were willing to show us more than just tolerance. At that moment, we felt like we belonged at this dance party in the dimly lit room, Motown music playing on: "Dancing in the Street" by Martha Reeves & The

Vandellas, "Ain't No Mountain High Enough" by Marvin Gaye & Tammi Terrell, "Stop! In the Name of Love" by The Supremes, "My Girl" by The Temptations.

We danced to the music with law students in a beautiful venue and suddenly felt older.

We sat down, and our new friends told us about the pressures of law-student life and how they came to the party to get away from the law for a while. But before we turned from the law, I did manage to get an explanation of those legal terms from the *Ideal Shoe Company* case: secured transactions, trover, and conversion. This knowledge oddly added to my appreciation of the night. And I began to think about the law. I didn't think asking them about the pornography case was a particularly good idea, so I asked whether they knew that Vernors originated in Detroit.

And after that, it seemed time for us to go.

My friend and I lingered outside in the Law Quad (after I took volume four hundred back to the library), discussing how we might actually describe this night to our friends at school on Monday. We were on a bench near the walls of the Law Quad's warm tan and beige Indiana limestone, which had absorbed over a half-century of discussions, explanations, and justifications. And, on that night, had housed a dance floor where three surprisingly sympathetic law students welcomed me into the fellowship of persons interested in the law.

CHAPTER 33
January 1976

A Carole King Concert

I PARKED AT THE CAMPUS CHAPEL and walked over to Hill Auditorium, just two blocks away, hoping that I could find my way into the Carole King concert. On the radio on the drive over, a newscaster had been analyzing President Ford's State of the Union address from earlier in this bicentennial year. "America is great because it is good," the president had repeated from past presidents. I repeated this phrase, and I knew that this concert would be good and great. But I didn't have a ticket.

I had driven over on the slippery roads in our family's last-choice car. It was a used purple Gremlin, a much maligned, small car manufactured by AMC Gremlin, and it looked absurd, as if the back had been cut off the assembly line too early at an abrupt 45-degree angle. Worse, it didn't do well in snow, so we had to put down the back seat and load a heavy tree trunk in the car along with heavy bags of sand. All to keep the car on the road in the winter. We all thought my dad had lost his mind when he came home with the car. "Have we paid for this already?" was all my mom said, looking at it from the back steps.

But the purple Gremlin got me to the concert that night.

I was thinking about all the music in Ann Arbor as I walked over to Hill. In addition to The Ark, the Canterbury House was also drawing in big names. There were large concerts at Crisler Arena. There was a Blues and Jazz Festival. There were concerts at West Park, until they got too loud and the city had to shut them down, and the Grateful Dead even played in West Park in 1967. And there were good club venues, like the Fifth Dimension and Chances Are, where I had heard Bob Seger and the Silver Bullet Band in 1975. It made me happy that Seger was from Ann Arbor and had been on the Ann Arbor High track team.

But the great thing about Hill Auditorium was that you could see classical performers of the day as well as folk and rock legends. The Berlin Philharmonic and Pink Floyd, Arthur Rubinstein and Joni Mitchell, Julian Bream and Bonnie Raitt. Renowned for its great acoustics, Hill Auditorium was viewed as a renowned concert hall since its opening in 1913.

And tonight, I was hoping just to get in. I scoped out the ticket takers in the entranceway, trying to detect the weakest link.

I approached my mark, "Hey, can I get in to see the rest of the show? I'll just stand in the back."

"Do you have a ticket?"

"No, I don't. I intended to buy one. I'm a big fan."

She busted my chops a bit, "You know, a lot of her fans took the further step of purchasing a ticket."

"Well, I wasn't sure I could make it tonight," I explained, "but I have *Tapestry*, and I would really like to see her."

She then looked at me so closely that it was as if she saw a ghost. "Did you clean the chapel down the street a while ago, when you were younger?"

I nodded.

"You've sure gotten tall."

I wasn't sure how to respond.

"You don't remember me, do you?" She paused and drew in a deep breath. She explained that she had stayed in the chapel basement for a time, was in a bad state, got money at the Hash Bash, and left for California.

"I think I gave you some money for helping me, and you said were going to get a Carole King album," she reminded me.

"Yes, I do remember you. I got that album."

Main Street at Night. With permission of Ken Cobb, Ann Arbor photographer.

She explained that she had made it to her sister's, got a job, and attended a community college. She then went to Berkeley and transferred back to U-M in the fall. Her former boyfriend never tried to catch up to her for the money. He died of a drug overdose just after she left for California.

"That was a good thing that he died, I have to admit," she said in a low voice, adding, "I'm in the music school. And take tickets for music events."

"Wow. Long time ago."

"I'm doing well now." She drew in a breath, "You know, I almost didn't get on that plane. But then I did. I swore that I would."

I said I was doing pretty well, except for the fact that I didn't have a ticket to the concert.

"What is that church word for random coincidences anyway?" she asked.

"Maybe 'providential'?" I suggested. She smiled.

"Well, come on through then, just keeping moving around the venue," she said, adding, "and if you get caught, don't tell them who let you in.

"Next time, buy a ticket," she laughed as I walked through.

The concert was a joyous celebration of life. I cheered as wildly as King's paying fans. Hearing Carole King sing "You've Got a Friend" as an encore convinced me that a girlfriend with a beautiful singing voice would be a good thing to have in 1976. I was sixteen now, and I would need to add this to an updated girlfriend list, as the prior list was almost two years old.

As much as I loved Carole King, I wasn't thinking about her for this role; she seemed unattainable. After the concert, as I was contemplating this thought on the steps of Hill Auditorium, I saw in the crowd a classmate from Pioneer choir and the school musical moving toward me with her friend.

"Great show, right?" she said. "I didn't know you were coming."

"I didn't know I was coming either," I replied, "I have a lot going on these days, with the play and all."

We talked on the steps of Hill Auditorium in the cold. She had a light blue coat and a red scarf; her glasses were steamed up in the cold. I then walked with my classmate and her friend through Ingalls Mall toward her car.

"See you at play practice tomorrow," she said as she left.

"I am working hard on the music."

She nodded.

We both knew that I needed a lot of practice.

186

CHAPTER 34
April 1976

The High School Musical

THE YOUNG WOMAN AT THE Carole King concert was the class-mate I had met in the library in tenth grade—the bibliophile. I eventually found out that her name was Chrissy, and she was the daughter of a U-M law professor.

We were in choir and American history classes together. Alongside these two classes, the school was also putting on an "Original Bicentennial Historical Musical." It was called *Ye Bloody Rebels*.

The musical was a historical love story set in Boston during the Revolution. The script and the music were written by Ann Arbor teachers. The play had a very large cast and required extra boys—of any ability—for the chorus and bit parts. And that is really the only explanation of how I ended up in A Capella Choir, the top choir, without having sung in choir before.

A subplot of the play was that three British officers fraternized with three friendly townswomen. Two boys and I were cast as British officers, and we were paired as singing and dancing partners with three young women. This group of six got to sing two songs, and we all got to wear elaborate costumes. The three young women were all kind, engaging, and excellent singers. The two other boys were also very good singers. I was not in the same category as the other five.

That fall, Chrissy encouraged my musical development. She had

PIONEER HIGH SCHOOL MUSIC DEPARTMENT

Presents

YE BLOODY REBELS!

AN ORIGINAL MUSICAL IN CELEBRATION OF
THE NATIONAL BICENTENNIAL, with book by
CAROL DUFFY, and music and lyrics by
DIANNE BAKER. Vocal arrangements by
JAMES W. BERG, orchestration by E. LOUIS SMITH.

April 1, 2, 3, 1976   8 P.M.
PIONEER HIGH SCHOOL AUDITORIUM,
ANN ARBOR

Ye Bloody Rebels Program, April 1976.

Chrissy and I fraternizing in *Ye Bloody Rebels*.

near-perfect pitch and great expression when she sang. She caught me by the elbow near her locker after a choir class that had ended with a particularly rousing version of the spiritual "Every Time I Feel the Spirit." I was swept away with enthusiasm. She said she hoped I wouldn't take this the wrong way: she appreciated my spiritedness, but she thought I should know …

"How far off tune?" I asked.

"Well, we will need to spend some very significant time together on this, if that is okay," she deflected.

And that was quite fine with me. We had been assigned as singing and dancing partners in the upcoming musical, and she promised to help me learn to sing in tune. And she did. We began to spend significant time together working on this musical, so if she began to turn toward me in choir or on stage, I knew how to adjust.

The fact that I ended up paired with her was not a certainty, as she was one of three possible young women. But before the actual pairing was done, I found myself walking into the music wing and entering the choir director's office to let him know my thoughts on this. With youthful impulse cloaked in what I thought seemed rational thinking, I focused on the theme of efficiency. Chrissy and I were already occasional American history study partners, and therefore it would be convenient for us to also be dance partners—"because it would be efficient," I said.

"Efficiency?" Mr. Pratt asked.

He was difficult to read. He seemed either amused or as though he was wondering exactly why he had let me into the choir in the first place. He denied having any role in the final pairing. But when I went to look at the posted list on the door of the choir rehearsal room the Monday after Thanksgiving, there it was: we were paired up. To this day, I don't know if Mr. Pratt intervened or if this was entirely random.

The play required us to hold hands, sit close to each other and talk, and sing to each other. For hours a day at rehearsal—all for academic credit. I couldn't wait to get to play practice every day. And I felt obligated to give thanks each day for the Ann Arbor public schools and the choir program.

We had to laugh at times at the odd circumstances in which we found ourselves. We were in 1976, dressed as characters from 1776, and in between scripted song and dance, we were, in fact, discussing American history assignments and studying for the AP American history test. In any event, what I had told Mr. Pratt turned out to be true: we did, in fact, use this time efficiently.

Act II, Scene 3, set in the town square, proved to be the highlight of my high school acting career. My major line as British Officer Howard was "I say. England doesn't want a war, and King George has been very generous with the colonies." I performed this line pretty well, though, in hindsight, the fact that I was indecisive as to whether to put the accent on "very" or "generous" was the likely cause of some hesitation in my delivery.

This line led immediately into a rousing song and dance number called (and it would be difficult to make this up) "Why Can't Those Rebels Be Reasonable?" It was the simultaneous singing and choreographed dancing—all while holding hands with Chrissy—that proved quite a lot for me to master. But I worked hard at it with her, and she was very charitable.

"You can do this," she said whenever I expressed any concerns.

Eventually, all this intense musical togetherness had to come to an end with the final performance. I found out that musical theater people were, perhaps, the most passionate people in high school, and cast parties involved a serious rush of emotions. At the end of a tremendous amount of coordinated energy and intense focus, it was now time to go back to a routine existence.

At the cast party, I wore denim overalls, my favorite blue-and-red checkered flannel shirt, and my Converse High Top basketball shoes. Standing outside the building, just beyond the dance area, Chrissy and I talked about the play. Stevie Wonder's "Signed, Sealed, Delivered (I'm Yours)" was playing inside.

With the gigantic moon overhead, she asked me what I would now do with all my free time since the play was over.

Despite time freezing, despite the leading question as large as the moon itself, despite the beat and the words of Stevie Wonder leading as bright as a neon sign, all I managed to reply was that I needed to catch up on my calculus homework, as I had fallen behind during the play. This memorable scene replayed over and over in my mind when I got home, and for the next week.

A gnawing realization of miscalculation crept over my entire being.

Calculus homework was not the answer Chrissy was seeking.

And it was not the right answer.

CHAPTER 35
April 1976

A First Date

I FINALLY RECALIBRATED. After class, I suggested to Chrissy that perhaps, if she wasn't doing anything more interesting, she'd like to see the movie *One Flew Over the Cuckoo's Nest* with Jack Nicholson— adding as a clincher—"to compare the movie to the book."

"Are you suggesting I go see it myself, or are you asking me to see this movie with you?" she asked.

I realized I had omitted that detail. "Yes, with me."

"So, you are rethinking your answer about your free time now that the play is over?"

I smiled sheepishly.

She asked if this was a literary event or more like a date.

I just said, "Yes."

The movie had gotten great reviews; one noted, "Adult Themes and Strong Language. Brief nudity." At sixteen, this seemed appropriate for a first-date movie. To be clear, the movie was Rated R, but I was technically underage, as you had to be seventeen to attend unless you went with your parents. However, the movie was at the Campus Theatre, so I assumed no one would actually check IDs, and this threshold concern faded quickly.

I had already given my mother the general details of the date but not the actual movie title or "R" rating. These details could easily have

Brother Tom in the family's Ford Fairlane, Fall 1976. By this time, the reverse gear was temporarily fixed.

caused parental inquisitional delay—all things to be avoided while getting dressed for a night in my best blue jeans, recently obtained Mansfield Relays t-shirt, and worn Adidas running shoes. And of course, my worn Levi's Jean Jacket.

I drove our old car, a two-door 1965 Ford Fairlane that had a huge front seat. Someone had gifted it to our family, and it could no longer go in reverse—admittedly a crucial function. It had to be driven and parked with great foresight. Rather than fix the car, my parents evidently thought that driving under these conditions would make us cautious and strategic drivers. But the car had a good radio, and Bob Seger accompanied me on the way—then Stevie Wonder, then Van Morrison. I was humming "Brown Eyed Girl" as I knocked on the big red door at her house in the Burns Park neighborhood. Three and a half miles from my house.

My classmate's father, a U-M law professor, answered the door, invited me in, and chatted with me. Things were going very well until he cross-examined me on whether I thought that "given the reviews, that you can actually get into this movie."

Time crystalized at that moment. I suspected that I might be in

Me (striped shirt), Tom, Sue, Mom, and the Ford Fairlane, Fall 1976. By this time, the reverse gear was temporarily fixed.

some sort of legal trap. I surmised that her father had read the reviews and seen the rating and realized that I was underage. Perhaps he was going to suggest an alternative to an adult-themed, strong-language-filled, brief-nudity-containing event.

Or it might be worse.

Suddenly, there sparked a further personal interest in law, as the following concerns crept into my mind: Was going underage to an R-rated movie with adult themes a criminal act? Did the use of a car to engage in this activity somehow heighten the criminal activity? Did a law professor have a special legal duty to report any act of social malfeasance to the police?

Wanting to avoid any legal entanglement, I weighed my words carefully. I looked down at the floor to get a grip on the situation but was immediately distracted: several of the green Adidas stripes had come loose from my right shoe and curled upwards. I had carefully glued them back into place earlier that morning, but it didn't stick.

I felt like I was coming apart at the seams from the shoes up. But I also thought what I needed was to simply provide the law professor with a more legalistic defense of the planned outing. What came out of my mouth next was a jumble of sentence fragments, and likely not even in this order: "Sir. Important book ... Read article in magazine. In the dentist office ... Movie ratings. Merely an industry standard. Not criminal. Not enforced ... Almost seventeen ... Law. I love the law."

There was a mirror in the hallway, and out of the corner of my eye, I surreally observed myself delivering these excited utterances.

Old-school, erudite, and taciturn Professor Cunningham, an expert on property law, administrative law, and regulatory law—who truly was wearing a sport coat and vest on an ordinary Saturday night at home—was clearly unable to decipher my jibber-jabber. I stood before him silently, fully denim clad, jiggling my right foot because the barely attached Adidas stripes were bugging me.

Taking pity on me, and in a dignified way, he clarified that he had recently read that the movie had won many awards and that he was merely suggesting that it may be crowded at the theater and thus hard to get into that night. A valuable lesson was learned then and there about listening very closely to a question before ever answering.

Fortunately, my classmate came down the stairs just then, wearing new white painter pants—obtained that morning from Sam's store downtown—and a paisley blouse she had made. She gracefully escorted me out the door before I could say another word to her father except "good night." And really, what else could I possibly have said at that moment? Confess that I was about to drive his youngest daughter in a defective car?

We watched the movie in the cramped theater and cheered Chief Bromden's escape from the mental institution at the end. As to the brief nudity that was warned about, I had evidently stepped out during that same brief moment to purchase Raisinets. Afterwards, my classmate did, in fact, point out some variations between the movie and the book.

After the movie, we went to the Lamplighter Restaurant on Liberty, a popular spot frequented by U-M football and basketball players. I had carrot cake and milk, and she had rice pudding and a Coke. Even though the drinking age was eighteen years old at the time, a lot of underage kids were drinking beer, as the enforcement was nonexistent at the Lamplighter. I chose milk because I favored it, and I was generally law-abiding, and I thought it might be tempting legal fate to order a beer—with carrot cake—so close in time to an underage, R-rated movie event.

"Did I hear correctly at my house that you were telling my father that you loved the law?"

"I'm not sure exactly what I told him," I said, unable to fully articulate what I had been saying while I had watched myself talk to him in a beveled part of a mirror.

"Do you know anything about law?"

"Quite a bit," I said, mentioning the U.S. Supreme Court's ruling in 1972 on the wiretapping of phones that arose out of a case in Ann Arbor. And I told her I had looked up federal cases in the fall in the U-M Law Library about obscenity, as well as secured transactions, trover, and conversion.

"What? Really?!" she exclaimed. "Definitely tell my father about this the next time we go out."

Next time.

We walked through the streets of Ann Arbor to my carefully parked car. By the University Diag, a fine mist and the palpable and pulsating press of spring embraced us. As she took my hand, the reality and unreality of that moment merged. We drew closer, and I noticed that the police and a tow truck were near where I had parked the car. They were in the process of towing away a car that had illegally parked in front of my car, wedging it in. I couldn't believe my good fortune. With her words "next time" still sinking in, at that moment, sixteen years old, the city and the future both seemed to provide profound promise.

And, like my car, we could only move forward.

CHAPTER 36
Summer 1976

Ann Arbor Libraries and a Suggestion

A COUPLE OF WEEKS AFTER my first date with Chrissy, hours after we took the AP American History test and minutes after we finished a pizza at Dominick's next to the Law School, I suggested we sneak into some libraries together. Growing up in Ann Arbor, the U-M campus was a playground, and it was always fun to slip into the campus libraries, through an unlocked door or past an inattentive security guard. Walking through the book aisles, watching the serious faces of the students, and feeling the vast information of the world around me: it was a thrill. Sneaking in simply added to that.

Chrissy paused at my suggestion and noted that this was certainly one option or—we could consider another.

"My father could get us research passes." She explained that she had just started working part-time for him as a research assistant.

"You mean a card that would allow us to get in anywhere in a legit way?" A startling and practical concept.

She got us passes, and we were legal, and we started to visit campus libraries. We began at the Clements Rare Book Library—one of her favorite places in the whole city. I confess that it was good to have the pass, but I was still glancing around for other ways to get in. It would certainly have been a challenge.

I always liked being around books. Growing up in Ann Arbor, I spent a great deal of time in libraries and bookstores. We were mainly a library family.

Our family went to the downtown public library twice a week—once, during the week, after swimming lessons at the YMCA across the street, smelling like chlorine—and then again on Saturdays. I got to know the layout well and the staff—particularly those staff members who allowed you to take out more than the eight books permitted at a time.

This limitation seemed horribly arbitrary, was something to scheme about at night, and was something that even prompted me at a young age to consider applying for a second card under an assumed name.

I had even decided on a first name: Wyatt, after the Western lawman Wyatt Earp. But I couldn't quite decide on a last name—either Earp or Postema or possibly two hybrids that I would concoct. There were pros and cons to each, but the internal debate went on for a while, and this plan stalled out.

And it became irrelevant in the summer. No school meant more reading time, so the public library had the public library bookmobile roll into our neighborhood once a week. The kindly driver of the giant RV-turned-portable-library didn't care how many books you took so long as you brought them back. And it was through the bookmobile that I learned of the social dimensions of books.

In the summer of 1967, I checked out the book *James and the Giant Peach* by Roald Dahl. In between the pages near the end of the book was a sheet of paper with a question on it: *"What do you like about this book? Please let me know with details."* It was signed with just a "T."

It also had instructions on where to put the book in the bookmobile—not in its proper place but a spot behind a very large book at the back near the top that had a great deal of dust on top of it and hadn't been checked out for years. This place and the book's identification numbers were given in the instructions on the sheet. So I filled it out, got into the bookmobile, and put this book in the secret location.

And waited.

Three weeks later, I was happy to find *James and the Giant Peach* back in the secret location, with comments on what I had written, and some follow-up questions. I answered them and added some questions of my own. This went back and forth a couple of times over the summer. The last note just said "thanks for writing" and that the note writer was moving to Texas the next day and that this would be the last note. Enclosed was a bookmark the person had made and a recommendation for another read: *The Hobbit* by J. R. R. Tolkien.

I wrote back, but I feared the person would already be gone. When the bookmobile came around for the last time at the end of the summer, I checked the secret location, and the book was gone. It was back in its proper location.

Over time, I expanded my range of book access, sneaking into the U-M libraries before Chrissy connected me with a research pass. And since she'd set me up, I wanted to repay her in kind with what I believed would be another good suggestion about reading.

I wanted to tell her about this at just the right time, one that arose eventually when we were on vacation. She had invited me to go on vacation to her grandparents' cottage on a river near the ocean. Going on a vacation with another family ... that just wasn't what our family did. We were expected to get a job for the summer and maybe go up north for a week in August as a family. And I had my summer job all lined up: student instructor at the Pioneer High School Basketball School, six hours a day in the hot gym for eight weeks—the program where I had perfected my game for many summers. Plus, I still had my lawn mowing customers.

Chrissy said she would talk to my parents. She did this rather abruptly at the end of a dinner at our house. "Mrs. Postema, I need your son for a week this summer," she explained, "to help our family with some work." She outlined that she needed me to come with her to work on her grandparents' property. There was lots of work to be done.

As I heard her frame this vacation as one involving physical labor, sounding exactly like a church service project, I could see that it was hitting a mark.

My mom said that it might be a good thing given all that had to be done at her grandparents' property.

Chrissy had never said that her grandparents were actually still alive—they had passed some years before. She had just said that their property needed the work. And that was true. The old house was perched on a hill over the river, with a hayfield and gardens between the river and the house. It smelled like box elder. I found out that we would have tasks from eight to noon: pulling weeds, haying a field, and picking strawberries, among others.

Before we left on vacation, Chrissy told me to bring some books along. We would be working in the morning, but she made it clear that she'd be reading from one to five.

As she sat next to the river and read, I'd gradually creep closer to her with a book, careful to keep quiet. And since I couldn't sit quiet the whole time, I would go out for a run.

Knowing she liked to read so much, I brought along what I assumed would be a welcome bit of information. I had seen an ad in the back of a magazine, a speed-reading course that cost two dollars. The ad promised that it could teach anyone to read thick novels in an hour or two.

Chrissy was a diligent reader. But I thought if she could read faster, she could increase the number of books she could read. Maybe double it. And because of this, her affection for me might also increase correspondingly.

This sounded like a good plan to the neural networks of a seventeen-year-old boy.

As she finished her reading period the first day, we were sitting at the edge of the dock, the tidal estuary bringing the tide in. I told her that I knew she loved to read and that I had something that might be able to help her. I told her about what I had learned from a course that I had purchased from an ad in a magazine.

The course suggested that the trick with novels was simply to skip over all the dialogue. Anything between quotation marks. And further, skip any interior dialogue of a character—that way you could get the gist of what was happening in the plot without getting bogged down in the details.

Her eyes widened as I spoke.

It was not from interest, I would learn. She said nothing initially but then suggested that I read her aloud some of the book she was currently reading: *One Hundred Years of Solitude*. I assumed this request was my initial reward for providing her this valuable information.

I read some of it out loud. And she asked me, then, to spend some special time on the dialogue and read it with the accents of the characters. And as I did this over the next couple of days, I finally caught on to what she was doing.

I was not stupid. I merely wanted to provide a solution to her for a problem that didn't even exist. Okay, I had made a truly stupid suggestion, and she was just making me read aloud until I understood this.

She could have sent me back home, and she could have laughed in my face, but instead, she believed in reading redemption and simply had me read some sense into myself. Aloud.

Embarrassment washed over me like the tidal estuary.

Wanting to salvage some modicum of pride, I asked whether I got any credit for the flawed suggestion I had made about speed-reading because it was made, in theory, just to increase her happiness.

"Not really," she said.

She also pointed out that there was something called "CliffsNotes," which just summarized a book and was available at Ulrich's for lazy college students. My mail-order suggestion was actually very inefficient compared to CliffsNotes. She even had a better solution for the problem she didn't have. In any case, we began reading out loud to each other that summer by the river. And when it got hot that afternoon, we dove into the river off the dock.

As I was in midair, reflecting on the ill-advised suggestion about speed-reading, I thought to myself, "She can keep me from such future foolishness."

Then we submerged ourselves in the river. We came up for air and looked at each other as if we were the only two people in the world.

And the water was wonderful.

CHAPTER 37
1976-1977

Senior Year: Ups and Downs

GOING INTO MY SENIOR YEAR of high school, President Ford was trailing Governor Jimmy Carter by a wide margin in the election polls. In November, Ford lost to Carter. And it was his own fault. While Ford thought pardoning Nixon for his crimes would help heal the nation, it didn't, and many of the nation's voters simply didn't forgive him for this. But Ford was from Michigan, so I felt his disappointment.

I had also begun to watch other elections. In April 1977, I watched the incumbent mayor of Ann Arbor, Albert Wheeler, win the mayoral election by a single vote. One vote. I was rooting for him, so I was relieved. My eighteenth birthday was a month after the election, so I couldn't vote, but I wondered what the disappointment would have been for the mayor if both my parents had been delayed any longer in getting to the polls to vote for him, which had almost happened.

And beginning that fall, I would have to face my own disappointments. I had a number of goals to achieve in my senior year of high school. In particular, I wanted to be the fastest distance runner in the state of Michigan. The prior spring, I had moved up to seventh in the state in the two-mile run. All of the runners ahead of me in the state the prior year had now graduated. So I thought the goal was attainable.

I trained extremely hard over the summer. I got a map of Ann Arbor, and I ran on every street in the city. Every night a new route—

sometimes with members of the team and sometimes by myself—watching the rhythms of life in Ann Arbor. Sometimes I would run seven miles round trip to Chrissy's house and back, early in the morning before work, just to spend ten minutes with her in her kitchen while she was drinking tea in her red robe.

On the weekend, I ran in the Arboretum. First, up and down the hill from the river to the Geddes Road entrance, then laps in the Arboretum Dow Prairie. Chrissy walked in the opposite direction with her dog in the prairie, and we smiled at each other when we passed. The long prairie grass swayed. She looked for the indigo buntings in the trees of the Arb at the edge of the meadow. We also walked on every path in the Arb together that summer after these runs.

But, in the end, my running dreams faded further that fall with each weekly meet. I got bronchitis and then developed some undiagnosed asthma issues that caused me to cramp up when running at a certain speed. Not enough oxygen, evidently. I had a season of struggle, and this was humbling; our team didn't qualify for the state meet. Even my best psych-up songs could not save me or propel me faster.

Neil Young provided inspiration for my hardships with "Long May You Run." Although I later found out the song was actually about a car, it soothed me: The lyrics talked about the shine of a chrome heart in the sun. And it encouraged a long run.

I never thought much about the chrome heart, as I thought it was just a variation of lyrics from his prior song, "Heart of Gold." A slightly less pure heart, I thought, but still very durable.

But I learned to persevere. I was co-captain of the team, and I was determined to lead that season. Not as someone at the front of a race but as someone leading through the long training miles around town with my teammates. And I continued to embrace those strides despite the struggle that continued through the spring track season.

After my trying cross-country season, in December, all my years of basketball practice yielded to another stark reality: my enthusiasm for the game of basketball could not compensate for my lack of true ability. Not only was I not on pace to play pro basketball like my hero Cazzie Russell, but I was also not good enough to even start on the varsity team and would likely be moving from second to third string.

Chrissy (in a handmade dress) and me, Senior Prom, May 1977.

I just had not played enough competitive basketball that summer, though I had been one of the student instructors at Pioneer High School Basketball Camp—just like my hero Bob Elliott. Except the kids got me, not a future NBA player. But teaching basketball to kids and playing basketball at a higher level were two different things. And there simply were others with more talent than me.

Not surprisingly, my playing time was minimal in the first two games of the season. So I went to the coach and told him I was going to leave the team to focus on running and salvage my running career. He made no effort to dissuade me.

But though the talent just wasn't there, nothing could take away the sheer joy that all my hours of basketball had provided: my teammates, the bus rides, the high-top Converse shoes, the struggles on the court, and the eternal hope of actually dunking a basketball. But running muscles are different than jumping muscles, and while I was getting closer to a dunk, it was simply not meant to be.

I had to let it all go.

One final disappointment was that I couldn't fit choir into my class schedule. No more musical outlet during the school day. No more spirituals. And no more practicing the annual Pioneer High School graduation hymn, "Battle Hymn of the Republic." The martial and religious words, meant to inspire the Northern troops in the Civil War to a righteous cause, would usher us into the battle of life, evidently. And I would not be in the choir to sing it that year.

With these disappointments, I needed to find some additional solace, purpose, and order in life.

As to solace, Chrissy had great handwriting and left me excellent notes of encouragement in the locker we shared near the biology classroom. We also decided to determine the best albums of the 1960s and 1970s, which involved careful listening and endless debate. And this was comforting. And finally, I began writing short stories, encouraged by an English teacher.

"How did you think of this crazy scenario?" she asked.

"I witnessed it on campus," was usually my response.

As to both purpose and order, I became somewhat obsessed with something called the "golden ratio": a ratio between two numbers that equals around 1.618. The Greek letter phi symbolized it, and it was related to the mathematical Fibonacci sequence. The golden ratio manifested itself in all sorts of ways in the natural world and had been observed by scientists at least since Leonardo da Vinci's time. And it was everywhere: the wings of moths and butterflies, sunflowers, and honeybees.

A divine proportion of simplicity and order.

For me, this obsession translated into a yearlong biology project concerning the geometric patterns of spiderwebs. Some spiders form their webs in logarithmic golden spirals, a variation of the golden ratio. I loaded our basement with old fish aquariums, each with three glass sides painted black. I put different types of spiders in them and looked at the various webs they made. I took pictures and measured angles and looked at ratios. Our science teacher Dr. Young—not Mr. Young—encouraged this obsession and told me to keep at it.

I bought tiny crickets at the pet store and kept them in a separate aquarium as a food source for the spiders. The lid was left off this aquarium one night, and the crickets escaped and dispersed in the basement. My mom came down into the basement to find me crawling on the floor, following the tiny chirps to recapture them.

She was unfazed. "Well, they really aren't hurting anything," she said.

Chrissy was also my biology lab partner, and we decided that, with her excellent handwriting, she would write up all our lab reports. I would write out the first draft in my scrawl, and then she would rewrite it into a final draft that looked excellent. Her project that year was on bird calls, so we went to various parks in town and listened to the birds.

She also made the college selection process pretty easy. I had always assumed I would go to the U-M, like my hero Cazzie Russell. However, about a month after our first date, near the end of junior year, she passed me a note in the back of history class. I had to sit up when I read the official-sounding introduction. "After careful consideration ..." it said. In sum, she thought it would be a good idea to go to college together. She gave me a list of four colleges she was going to apply to.

At seventeen, getting some direction was great. As much as she loved Ann Arbor, she wanted to go away to college. So I told her to give me her top two colleges and I would apply to them. I listened to the words of Carole King's "Where You Lead." Following my smart girlfriend, a bibliophile, seemed like a good idea. So she gave me her top two picks.

In the fall, I set to work on the college applications. As it happens, I wrote a generic essay on things I had observed when running through my hometown. Not a terribly original or deep topic, but it was certainly flexible, and I used it no matter what the essay topic was—often for multiple essays in the same application.

This strategy paid off.

In April, we went to the post office downtown and mailed in our college acceptances, then walked through the University of Michigan campus realizing we would soon leave our city for another great college town. Together.

We graduated on a hot night in June at Crisler Arena, The House that Cazzie Built, the venue of many great concerts in Ann Arbor. Elvis Presley had sung one of his last concerts here the prior month.

Our graduation from public school in secular Ann Arbor surprisingly included both a religious Invocation and Benediction. And, to add a further dose of military righteousness, the class hymn echoed throughout Crisler Arena:

Mine eyes have seen the glory of the coming of the Lord;

He is trampling out the vintage where the grapes of wrath are stored;

He hath loosed the fateful lightning of His terrible swift sword:

His truth is marching on.

Although I was not in A Capella Choir anymore, I knew the song well, and I sang along for good measure. Trampling grapes of wrath somehow appealed to me, particularly if I could run while doing it.

During the song, my mind wandered for a minute, and I counted the chairs that had been set up for our class on the arena floor. Essentially, thirty-two rows across by twenty deep. Chairs for our class of over six hundred students. I got out a pen and made a quick calculation on the program. The chair row width-to-depth ratio was 1.6—approaching the golden ratio. This gave me a strange satisfaction.

And while some of my classmates had gotten high before the graduation ceremony, the graduation scene was entirely surreal to me without drugs: strange and dreamy, hot and humid, coming in and out of focus. Under my graduation robe, I was wearing a very large bow tie that didn't fit well, but that my mom had bought at Bargain Days the prior summer just for this occasion.

I was grateful for the education I had received and my classmates. And we were being released into the world that night, sitting in rows approaching a golden ratio, in a sea of purple caps and gowns, the words of the "Battle Hymn of the Republic" ringing out in Crisler Arena: Truth is marching on.

And I could only do one thing at that moment.

I sang along with more of the refrain:

"Glory, glory, hallelujah."

Nickels Arcade. Looking out towards the Diag. With permission of Ken Cobb, Ann Arbor photographer.

EPILOGUE

I LEFT ANN ARBOR FOR COLLEGE in the fall of 1977, not knowing if I would ever return to live there again. My parents drove me to college in September in our family station wagon. I had a used Smith Corona typewriter, a calculator, a small clock radio, running shoes, basketball shoes, one suitcase, one duffel bag, and one suit. It was a new tan corduroy suit (and matching vest) that my mom had found at Bargain Days.

As to the light blue typewriter, my mother had found the advertisement for it in the classifieds. She went to take a look at it and was gone a long time. She sat with the woman selling it and found out that her son had taken it to college the year before. He passed away that year. She had no doubt consoled this woman.

My mom sat me down and, in her firm and resolute way, with her tears held back, emphasized, "It is really important to write a lot of good papers and stories on this typewriter."

"You understand why. To give honor to this boy."

This added some pressure.

Before I left, I had to attend to things in Ann Arbor over the summer. I sold my drum set to make money for college. And I got a summer job as a janitor at the University of Michigan hospital, cleaning in the children's ward, maternity ward, and delivery room. I worked the 7:30 a.m. to 3:30 p.m. shift, and sometimes the next shift also, at time and half pay.

As I had been a janitor since 1971, I had plenty of experience. I cleaned up every color and variation of liquid and solid produced by the human body that summer. I took great pride in cleaning at the hospital. One of the nurses also thought I would benefit from viewing a few live births that summer. She arranged for me to come in with her as a medical student. "Student of medicine in the broader sense," she said.

"Look, you will be the only one in your college class to have seen this," she explained, adding, "if you ever need to deliver a baby in an emergency, you'll be fully prepared." That certainly made sense to me.

I also had to train my sister Carol to take over janitorial duties at the chapel. I gave her my stereo too.

I ran the streets of Ann Arbor in the evenings, preparing to go out for the cross-country team in college. This allowed me additional time to survey my city.

I also brought to college, in my mind, a collage of the rhythms of life witnessed on Covington, in Ann Arbor, and in Michigan. The red leather chair and the gaze of Martin Luther King Jr.; Cazzie Russell, tube socks, gyms, duct tape, Officer Fleming.

And the images continued: baked goods, salted black licorice, Stevie Wonder, Lutheran School hot lunch, my friends and confidants, geometry, The Ark, Jarts, my peace-sign ring, my large hunting knife, cleaning the Campus Chapel, selling screwdriver kits on the Diag, the bookmobile, student protests, Pioneer Basketball School, the Pioneer track.

All these thoughts—and all my running around town—prepared me to leave.

And prepared me to introduce myself at college: "Hello, I'm from Ann Arbor, Michigan."

I returned to Ann Arbor in the summer of 1981 with my college diploma in hand. I had gone to Harvard University with Chrissy.

We lived in Cambridge for a year after college, while we both worked at Harvard. I had obtained some direction by that time and planned to attend law school in Madison, Wisconsin—another excellent college town. My father-in-law, Professor Cunningham, had encouraged my interest in law.

My father officiated our wedding in Ann Arbor at St. Andrew's Episcopal Church, where my mother-in-law tended the gardens. We then spent three years in Madison, Wisconsin, where I attended law school. My wife loved books and worked in publishing.

As much as I liked Cambridge and Madison, when I finished law school, I knew I would return to Ann Arbor, which we did in 1985. My parents still lived on Covington and her parents still on Copley. I began my legal career there, clerking for a federal judge—a good friend of federal judge Damon Keith, the initial judge of the Supreme Court wiretap case. I became a trial lawyer and was a partner in a large state-wide law firm. My years of memory work and recitation in class prepared me well for a career in law.

We raised four children in the Eberwhite neighborhood. In 2003, the City of Ann Arbor found itself in serious legal trouble, and I was asked to apply to become the City Attorney. Chrissy encouraged me to do this. I told the City Council that I knew every square inch of the city, that I was grateful for the opportunities the city had provided to me, and that I would take good care of the city. And I did, serving for nineteen years.

When I retired, I told the City Council and the audience: "I stand before you with a sense of accomplishment, with the knowledge of the flow of history in this city over the past nineteen years, with the knowledge of the work that was needed and that was done, and ultimately, I am here with a sense of optimism for the future."

And that was difficult to say, as my wife Chrissy could not attend my final city council meeting because she was in the midst of a cancer battle. She encouraged me to write this book several years ago. It started with stories I told to my family, and then told in speeches as the City Attorney. I posted some on a website for people who grew up in Ann Arbor.

Then I wrote these short essays. I had finished most by the time Chrissy passed away in January 2024. One of the last things she made me promise was to finish the rest of them and publish them, to capture a small slice of the history in Ann Arbor.

History, when the white oak near my house on Covington was only around two hundred years old. When the music of the 1960s and the 1970s shaped our lives. When the promise of Ann Arbor seemed endless.

So, I have written about the time and place in history that we shared.

When we were young.

And we spent our time running around town.

ACKNOWLEDGMENTS

This book was a labor of love, and many people encouraged me to write. First, my late wife Chrissy who patiently reviewed the first twenty-five essays and bluntly and kindly assessed these pieces, and others that didn't make the cut.

My daughter Tess took over initial editing after Chrissy passed. She inherited her mother's keen editorial sense and love of words.

My children Ben, Jake, Tess, and Elizabeth and my siblings Tom (and Michele), Carol, and Sue listened and then read some of these essays over time and fact-checked me on a number of matters. Some family factual matters remain in serious dispute.

My father, Don Postema, read through an early version of the book, as did Pioneer High School classmate and Ann Arbor journalist Geoff Larcom. They both provided great insights into Ann Arbor and these decades.

Friends from junior high school, high school, and college encouraged me to complete this book, or read chapters, listened to me read chapters, and provided information and comments, including: Faith Carroll, Kathy Scarnecchia, Victoria Powers, Ed Bostic, Ben Slote, Victor Drake, Carl Warschausky, Carol Thrane, Steve Thiry, Julie Vosper, David Jacobi, Walter Gillett, Bill Rose, Mike Gilson, and Martha Lawless.

I posted some of these essays on the website "Ann Arbor Townies," and people commented on them, gave me ideas, and wrote to me about Ann Arbor. And so, I have been able to correspond with people across the country about crazy or funny or special things that happened to them in Ann Arbor.

I am appreciative of the *Ann Arbor Observer* editor John Hilton, who published a version of "Middle Earth and a Peace Sign Necklace" in the November 2024 edition.

Finally, the staff at Fifth Avenue Press has been diligent and helpful, including copy-editor Walker, graphic artist Nate Pocsi-Morrison, and editor Emily Murphy. Emily worked diligently with me on this project. Further, her work on this book deserves an explanation. I was working on the book in February 2024, looking out on the Pacific Ocean in Laguna Beach, California. It was pouring rain, and I had a mental block on the rewrites to the chapter on 1810 Covington. I got an email from Emily, introducing herself as the editor assigned to my project, asking how I was coming along on it.

She also said, in closing, that she wanted to see this project published, as she lived at 1810 Covington. Her husband had bought the house from my parents in 2016, when they sold the house after living there for fifty-three years. Emily moved in some years later. Well, this coincidence prompted me to sit up and get typing that day immediately. And Emily kept me on task in 2024 and 2025.

ABOUT THE AUTHOR

Stephen K. Postema is a graduate of Ann Arbor Schools, Harvard University, and the University of Wisconsin Law School. He served as the Ann Arbor City Attorney from 2003 to 2022. He is a practicing lawyer in downtown Ann Arbor, a mediator, and a writer and speaker on legal topics. The summer of 1976, he ran on every street in Ann Arbor, just because he wanted to.